COPTIC ORTHODOX
PATRIARCHATE

MANY YEARS

WITH PEOPLE'S QUESTIONS

PART II

Theological & Dogmatic Questions

By

H.H. POPE SHENOUDA III

Title:	Many Years with the People's Questions Part II
Author:	H. H. Pope Shenouda III.
Translated by:	Dr. Wedad Abbas.
Illustrated by:	Sister Sawsan.
Typesetting:	El-Nasekh El-Saree Computer, (Delta Branch).
Press:	Dar El-Tebaa El Kawmia, Cairo.
Edition:	First - April 1995.
Legal Deposit No.:	2624 / 1995
Revised:	COEPA - 1997

H.H. Pope Shenouda III
117th Pope and Patriarch of Alexandria
and the See of St Mark

Table of Contents

Introduction
1. Does Man Have A Free Will Or Not?
2. Why Did God Create Man?
3. Is Conscience God's Voice?
4. Madness and Accountability For Sins
5. Does The Body Sin Alone?
6. Do Human Beings Get Married To Devils And Procreate?
7. Does The Holy Spirit Work In The Unbelievers?
8. When Did The Disciples Receive The Holy Spirit?
9. Is There A Gospel Of St. Paul The Apostle?
10. What Is The Difference Between Christ As Son Of God And Us As Children Of God?
11. Adam And The Lord Christ.
12. Why - After Salvation - Do Men Toil And Women Conceive in Pain?
13. Why Did We Not Die Immediately After Sinning?
14. Why Do We Die Though Salvation Has Been Effected?
15. Our Attitude Towards The Lord Christ's Blood
16. How Can He Die Though He Is God?
17. How Did The Lord Christ Die While His Divinity Was Not Separated From His Humanity?

18. The Body Of The Lord Christ In The Church And Eucharist.
19. Saturday & Sunday.
20. Why Do We Baptise Babes Who Have Not Yet Believed?
21. Why Do One Sin After Renewal In Baptism?
22. Can A Blessing Be Taken From A Human?
23. The Holy Trinity of Christianity And The So-Called Trinity Of Heathen.
24. Does Incarnation Mean Limitation?
25. Is Christ For Jews Only?
26. What Does Sitting On The Right Of The Father Mean?
27. What Is The Meaning Of Partakers Of The Divine Nature?
28. Have Christ's Miracles been Worked By Impression?

29. Did Christ Work His Miracles by Prayers?
30. Is The Title "Son Of Man" Against Christ's Divinity?

31. Spiritualism.
32. May The Devil Be Saved?
33. Those Whom The Church Does Not pray For.
34. Those Who Were Forgiven Before The Cross.
35. How Can It Be That Christ Prays And Gets Tired?

INTRODUCTION

When I thought of printing the collection, "So Many Years With The Problems Of People", I found before me thousands of questions I had answered throughout more than twenty years. I classified them into sections according to topics.

Part I of the collection includes questions on the Holy Bible.

It contained forty questions often addressed by many. Some were answered briefly and the others with some elucidation, but in both cases with much concentration.

The first part was out of print and was reprinted before printing this second part.

This Second Part includes theological and dogmatic questions that occupy the minds of the people. We tried to tackle them in an easy way as far as possible so that everyone may understand them. However, we still have enough theological and biblical questions for many books.

We hope that this collection will be beneficial and convey the message, especially among the youth, in the service and to the students of the religious institutes as well as to whoever wants to know the answers to these questions.

Pope Shenouda III

(1)

DOES MAN HAVE A FREE WILL OR NOT?

Question:

Does man have a free will or not? And if he does, is it for everything?

Answer:

There are certain matters which man has no choice.

A person has no choice regarding the country in which he was born, the people amidst whom he grew up, the parents who brought him into existence, the environment in which he was brought up and its impact on him, nor the way he was brought up.

His shape or colour, his height, intelligence, the talents he is endowed with or deprived of, what he inherited from his parents ... etc.

On the other hand a person no doubt has free will with respect to his actions and works.

He has the choice either to do something or not, or to speak or to keep silent. He can even - if he wants - correct many things which he inherited and change what he acquired from the environment or while being brought up.

A person can set aside the whole past and begin a new life completely different, getting rid of all previous influences.

Many people were able - when they grew up to release themselves of the influence of the environment, education and inheritance which they had undergone in their childhood. They could do this by bringing themselves into the scope of new, different influences through reading, friendship and company, spiritual guides and new teachers or through religious life and meetings. There are actually some people who were brought up in a dissolute life but repented; and others who were brought up in spirituality yet they deviated.

Even with respect to talents ...

A person can develop the talents with which he was born, or diminish them by neglecting them. Someone may have only few talents which he is careful to improve and protect, so they develop. Another may acquire new talents which he had not and become better than one with talents which are neglected.

Many things prove that man has free will:

1. The existence of God's commandment is a proof that man has a free will.

If a man is directed and has no control over his will or freedom, why would there be a commandment? And what would be its use if a person is unable to comply with or is directed against it involuntarily? We remember here some words of a part which apply to this:

He was cast into the water with hands tied and he was warned not to get wet!

Even if a person is directed in the way which the commandment requires him to walk, the commandment will not be necessary since he will walk that same way whether there is a commandment or not!

It is logical then that since there is a commandment, man has free will. He has the choice either to follow God's commandment or not. This is also the actual state of affairs which we see in life. A person is able to obey the commandment if he wants to and can disobey if he wants. God has endowed him with a free will and a free choice. God is put in his sight, but he is not forced to go along it.

2. The existence of sin is a proof that man has a free will.

If man has no free will, would it be reasonable that God leads him to sin? Would not that mean that God participates with man in committing sin? God forbid. It is unreasonable and does not conform with God's nature as Holy and good, hates evil and does not accept it, but calls all people to repent and forsake sin.

When sin exists, it means that man has done it voluntarily by his own will while he had the choice to commit it or not.

If man has the free will to do evil, he is rather more free to do good and free to repent and forsake sin. God calls all people to repent, but leaves the matter to their choice either to repent or not.

3. The existence of a condemnation is a proof that man has free will.

Mere existence of punishment and reward is a proof that man is free to do whatever he wants; for the simplest rule of justice necessitates that no man may be condemned unless he is apt, free and willing. If a person is proved to have no choice or will, he will not be condemned nor justified; for no responsibility is there in the case of lack of free will.

Accordingly, God cannot condemn a sinner with eternal torment unless such a person has full choice and chose for himself bad conduct and walked in it, so he reaps the fruit of his choice and work and as far as a person has control over his will his punishment will be.

God never punishes a person who has no free will for he has no control over his will, but punishes him who led that person to sin. The same principle applies to reward; God rewards the person who does good voluntarily, by his own will and choice. If such a person has no free will, he will not deserve to be rewarded.

4. Finally, there are four remarks:

First: God urges everyone to do good and guides him to avoid wrongdoing whether through one's own conscience, through guides, fathers and teachers and through the work of grace.

Yet God leaves to everyone the choice to accept or refuse.

Second: Sometimes, God interferes to stop certain evils and prevents some doing them. In this case, the person who was prevented from doing evil has no hand in this and will not be rewarded. Here God - for the sake of general benefit undertakes the matter or turns evil to good. As for the other affairs of a person and his conduct, he has the choice and the will.

Third: A person may lose his will by his own choice, such as when he submits to a certain sin by his own will until the sin becomes a habit or another nature to him which he follows afterwards as if he has become without any will.

It is in fact lack of will caused by a previous action taken by a person with his free will and choice.

Fourth: God will condemn everyone on the last day according to the reason and discretion endowed him by God and according to his capabilities, his will and choice. God takes into consideration man's circumstances and the pressures he faces as well as his ability or non ability to overcome such pressures.

(2)

WHY DID GOD CREATE MAN?

Question:

**Why did God create man?
Did he create man to worship and glorify Him?**

Answer:

God did not create man to worship and glorify Him; for God does not need any glorification or worship from man. Before creating man, God was glorified and worshipped by the angels and even then He was not in need of being glorified by the angels. He is glorified by His own attributes.

God lacks nothing to acquire from His creation whether man or angel.

How true this is expressed in the Mass written by St. Gregory, in which man prays to God, saying, "you were not in need of my servitude, but it is I who am in need of Your Lordship."

Why then did God create man?

God created man out of His goodness and munificence, in order to make man enjoy existence.

Before creation, God was alone. Since eternity He was the only being in existence and had satisfaction in Himself. It was possible that man does not exist nor any other creature, but God out of His munificence and goodness granted existence to this nothingness which He called man. He created man to enjoy existence.

Creating man was then for the benefit of man himself not for the benefit of God. He created man to enjoy life and if he behaves well he will also enjoy eternity.

The same can be said regarding angels. God was so bountiful that He made us part of existence which He would have been alone in it. It is impossible that God created man because He desired to be glorified by that man or any other creation.

When we glorify God, it is we, not God, who benefit.

We benefit because when we mention God's name and give glory to Him, we raise our hearts to a spiritual level which gives our hearts elevation, purity and closeness to the Godhead. We need always to contemplate on God and glorify Him; for by this our spirits feel connected to this great God who has all such glory and this gives us comfort.

Therefore we say, "It is I who am in need of Your Lordship."

On the other hand, God - theologically speaking - does not increase or decrease in greatness. Nothing is added to Him when we glorify Him and He lacks nothing when we do not.

I can say that God created us out of His love for us as His pleasure is in the human beings.

God loved us before we existed and that is why He brought us into existence.

But what do the words "loved us before we existed" mean?

This reminds me of what I wrote in my notebook in 1957 as far as I remember, I wrote: "I have a relation, O Lord with you which began since eternity and will continue for ever. Yes, I dare say it began since eternity! I mean since eternity when I was in Your mind a thought and in Your heart a pleasure."

(3)

IS CONSCIENCE GODS VOICE?

Question:

Is conscience God's voice?

Answer:

No, conscience is not God's voice, because conscience often errs whereas God's voice never does.

The best evidence of this is found in the words of the Lord Christ to His disciples, for He said to them, *"They will put you out of the synagogues; yes, the time is coming that whoever kills you will think that he offers God service." (John 16:2).* Of course such conscience which considers killing the disciples is a worship offered to God can never be God's voice. This is just an example of many other cases.

Conscience might be strict and suspicious, thinks a thing sinful while it is not, or has an exaggerated look to sin. Conscience might also be lenient, accepts many wrong things and justifies them. Neither of these two kinds of conscience - that which strains out a gnat or which swallows a camel - (Matt 23:24) can be God's voice.

When a person murders someone to avenge for killing his brother or father and his conscience becomes troubled until he avenges for the blood of his relative, this conscience cannot be God's voice. Likewise a person who kills his sister for committing adultery to cleanse the name of the family cannot claim that he was called by God's voice to kill her.

Some people mix up between conscience and the Holy Spirit.

God's voice within a person is the voice of God's Spirit working within him and thus it cannot err. On the other hand, conscience can be mistaken; for sometimes a person gets enthusiastic to do something and his conscience irritates him for not doing it while God's Spirit is in fact not pleased by such action.

Conscience may develop when instructed and guided.

It can discern today that the thing it deemed allowable yesterday due to ignorance or misunderstanding is in fact forbidden. Can it (conscience) be God's voice while it judges matters differently from one day to another? The changing of conscience is an evidence that it is not God's voice.

A person may, in the name of mercy and compassion, help a student to cheat in the exam when he sees him crying for fear of failure, or a physician, in the name of mercy and compassion, may write a certificate that someone is sick while in fact such a person is not sick. Afterwards, he is instructed that what he has done was wrong and refuses to do it again in future.

How then can such conscience be God's voice in man while it calls for something and on another occasion calls for something else?

Another example is a person who is urged by his conscience to obey some spiritual father or guide even in doing something wrong, but afterwards he understands that such obedience should be within obedience to God. His conscience rebukes him for his previous obedience by which he broke God's commandment.

Conscience is a voice put by God in man to call him to do good and reprimand him for wickedness, but is not God's voice.

God put also in man a mind to invite him to good.

He gave man a spirit which covets against the body.

However, the mind often does wrong and the spirit also often errs.

Both are from God, but not God's mind nor God's voice.

God's voice in man is the Spirit of God working within man.

(4)

MADNESS AND ACCOUNTABILITY FOR SINS

Question:

To what extent can a mad person be held accountable for his sins? Or is he accountable at all?

Answer:

It is well known that according to one's aptness and discerning one is held accountable by God.

Madness is of various degrees and types. There may be a person who is mad with regard to a certain subject and in other cases he behaves as if he is completely sane so that those who do not know him will never imagine that he is mad. There is also a kind of madness which is not continuous, of which a person can be cured but returns again. Another kind is sheer madness or absolute madness in which the mind is totally insane.

A person who is absolutely mad cannot be held accountable for anything at all.

He is not charged for any sin he commits while being mad because he is not aware.
He is only charged for the sins he committed before getting mad, after which time he is considered dead and is not held accountable.

With regard to other kinds of madness he is charged as far as he is discerning and as far as he is able to control his behaviour.

Seeing that the Lord has said about those who crucified Him, *"Father, forgive them, for they do not know what they do " (Luke 23:34)*, how much rather the mad should be forgiven; for mentally "they do not know what they are doing".

(5)

DOES THE BODY (THE FLESH) SIN ALONE?

Question:

Is the body the element of sin in a person? Is it the cause of all sins? Is it accountable for sins so as it might be called the body of sin? Does it sin alone and the spirit has no hand in the matter because what the spirit desires is opposed to the flesh (Gal 5:17)?

If so, why did God create the flesh?

Answer:

If the flesh had been evil in itself, God would have not created it.

We observe that after creating man, flesh and spirit, *"God saw everything that He had made, and indeed it was very good. So the evening and the morning were the sixth day."* *(Gen 1:31)*. So, God did not create the flesh as an element of sin. Adam and Eve lived in the body in Paradise without sinning; they lived in simplicity, chastity and innocence before sin entered into the world.

We cannot say that the body began with sin!

It is true that the fruit was forbidden and they ate from it, but before eating there was the lust for divinity, the lust for knowledge and doubting God's words (which are all sins of the spirit). The enticement of the serpent was clear, "You will not die." Thus began doubting God's words. There was also the enticement of divinity, *"you will be like God, knowing good and evil " (Gen 3:5)*. Would it be that the spirit coveted after divinity and knowledge and it let the body fall with it and eat from the fruit? Perhaps, or at least we can say:

The first man's fall was a fall of the flesh and spirit together.

Both joined together in one action, i.e. breaking God's commandment.

However, most people speak only about the sin of the body which took the fruit and ate it, forgetting the inner factors that led to this which are sins of the spirit. The spirit can sin the same as the body and we should not say that the body sins alone.

Moreover, the first sin known in the world is a sin of the spirit.

We mean the sin of the devil; for he is a spirit without flesh being an angel and the angels are spirits (Ps 104:4). The devil fell in the sin of pride when he said, *"I will ascend into heaven, I will exalt my throne above the stars of GOD... I will be like the Most High..'" (Is 14:13,14)*.

The first sin is pride and it is a sin of the spirit.

In the case of the devil, it was followed by obstinacy, resistance and stumbling others.
He made other angels fall, then he made man stumble. These were all sins of the spirit without the body.

The devil fell also in the sin of envy as we say in the Holy Divine Mass, "The death which entered into the world by the envy of the devil, You have abolished".

The devil - though a spirit - fell also in the sin of lying as he lied to Eve and the Lord said about him, *"He is a liar and the father of it." (John 8:44)*.

The spirit then can sin alone without the body.

Not all the sins of the spirit lie in its submission to the flesh. Nay, there are sins in which the spirit falls alone. The body might fall with the spirit, taking part in these sins. But with respect to the devil, all the aforementioned sins were sins of the spirit alone.

We should not say that the flesh is the cause of all sins.

There are many sins in which the spirit falls and we even say that the flesh alone without the spirit cannot sin. Like a dead body which takes life from the spirit, the spirit takes part in the sins of the body by submitting to it. Take for example the sin of killing. Do you think that the flesh alone attacks, beats and kills, or rather the sins of the spirit such as hatred and violence urge it to do so? Cain fell with the spirit before murdering his brother with his hand.

Being aware of the sins of the spirit and the soul, we pray in the Holy Mass, saying, "Purify our souls, our bodies and our spirits".

And we say that we partake of the Holy Communion "A purification for our souls, our bodies and our spirits".
And because the spirit like the body may be defiled and become unclean we say in the third hour prayer:

"Purify us from the defilement of the flesh and the spirit".

Since the spirit sins with the body, it will therefore be punished with the body in eternity so as the body is not punished alone.

If the spirit were strong, it would not fall in its own sins nor submit to the body in its sins. The most awful description given in the Holy Bible to the spirits of the fallen angels is the term "unclean spirits" or "evil spirits" as in (Matt 10:1). How much rather this description can be given to the spirits of the evil human beings.

The problem with the body is that it is made of material and so it is fought by being attracted to it.

It is fought with material and fleshly things and has more occasions which make it fall; for many are the fields in which it is fought. However, it is not necessarily subject to the material; it can be elevated over it.

For all these and the alike we honour the relics of the saints.

Their bodies struggled for God's sake, suffered for Him, lived in chastity, conquered the enemy and took part in every worship. They are honoured not only by us, but also by God Himself who allowed that a dead man comes to life on touching the bones of Elisha the Prophet (2 Kin 13:21).

The Lord so honoured the body that He made it a temple of the Holy Spirit.

The apostle therefore said, *"Or do you not know that your body is a temple of the Holy Spirit." (1 Cor 6:19)*.

Can we say then that this temple of the Holy Spirit is the body of sin? God forbid. The apostle says further, *"Do you not know that your bodies are members of Christ." (1 Cor 6:15)*.

The bodies then are holy and the words of the apostle are well said,

"..your body is a temple of the Holy Spirit ... which you have from God ... therefore glorify God in your body." (1 Cor 6:20).

We can thus glorify God with our bodies as well as with our spirits, *"always carrying about in the body the dying of the Lord Jesus, that the life of Jesus also may be manifested in our body." (2 Cor 4:10).*

Our bodies which we took from the Lord in baptism is not the body of sin; for the apostle says, *"For as many of you as were baptised into Christ have put on Christ." (Gal 3:27).*

God will honour the body when He will raise it in glory.

The body will rise imperishable, a spiritual shining body with a glorified nature like the body of His glory.

The greatest honour for the human body is that Christ took on Himself a human body.

If the body had been evil in itself or an element for sin, Christ would not have taken for Himself a body of our same nature blessing our nature in it.

The body may sin and may also live in purity.

The same applies to the spirit. We cannot forget also that when the body - though being material - overcomes material attraction and behaves in a spiritual way. God will not forget this loving fatigue and will consider it a great thing.

Let us then glorify God in our bodies and in our spirits which are from God.

(6)

DO HUMAN BEINGS GET MARRIED TO DEVILS AND PROCREATE?

Question:

Some people tell stories about human beings married to devils giving birth to children. To what extent is this correct? And how did they come to know of it?

Answer:

We do not believe this at all. It is not supported by any creed or historical evidence.

We do not know of any person descending from the devils. It is something unreasonable and can be refuted on basis of faith. Among the refutations we mention the following:

The devils are spirits having no bodies to procreate like human beings.

Devils are spirits because they are angels and they are called spirits in the Holy Bible (Luke 10:17,20).

They are even called "unclean spirits" (Matt 10:1) and "evil spirits" (Luke 7:21; Ac 19:12). How then can spirits procreate? And how, without having bodies, can they produce an offspring having bodies?

Of course sexual relations and marriage have no existence among these spirits.

The devils, though they lost their holiness, still have the angelical nature. That is why it is written in the Revelation that a war broke out in heaven between Michael and his angels and the dragon and his angels. They fought, *"So the great dragon was cast out, that serpent of old, called the Devil and Satan, who deceives the whole world, he was cast to the earth and his angels were cast out with him." (Rev 12:7-9)*.

And whereas they are angels, see what the Lord Christ said about the angels when speaking about the Resurrection. He said, **"*For in the resurrection they neither marry nor are given in marriage, but are like angels of God in heaven." (Matt 22:30)*.**

Angels do not marry and this applies to the devils as they are angels. The devils may arouse sexual feelings in human beings but they themselves do not have such sexual nature. The devil may appear in the form of a man or a woman, however:

There are no males nor females among the devils. They do not have bodies of men or women, nor do they have ovum or sperms. They cannot give a human offspring nor even a devil offspring. The devils are great in number because of the great number of the fallen angels not because of procreation among themselves. If they do not procreate among themselves, how can they procreate from human beings!

Moreover, procreation needs conformity of kind or species.

For example, no procreation can take place between a fish and a bird, a bird and an animal, nor between an animal and a fish nor between a human being and a bird. There must be conformity in sex and kind. Accordingly, no procreation can take place between a human being and a devil. Besides, a devil has no body.

History has not presented to us even one example of such procreation.

We have not heard of any person born of parents; one of them a human being and the other a devil, so that such a person might give us an answer to the confusing question: Which of the two natures prevails in such a relation, so that the offspring might be either a human being or a devil, or even a human-devil! Would such a being be visible or not!

Perhaps such questions are due to the stories of demons told to children and regretfully fill the children's libraries. Add to this the stories spreading among the common people and villagers who circulate these stories forming of them an important part of their folklore.

(7)

DOES THE HOLY SPIRIT WORK IN THE UNBELIEVERS?

Question:

In the story of the baptism of Cornelius while Peter was speaking, "The Holy Spirit fell upon all those who heard the word." This made the believers astonished, *"Because the gift of the Holy Spirit has been poured out on the Gentiles also" (Acts 10:44,45).*

Does this mean that the Holy Spirit works in the unbelievers?

Answer:

The Holy Spirit works in the unbelievers to make them believe.

Or how can they believe without the work of the Holy Spirit in them? Does not the Holy Bible say, *"No one can say that Jesus is Lord except by the Holy Spirit" (1 Cor 12:3).*

The work of the Holy Spirit to make people believe differs from His permanent dwelling in a believer.

The Holy Spirit may work in the heart of an unbeliever to call him to believe, or work a miracle or some wonder to him which might lead him to believe, but after believing, a person must obtain the Holy Spirit through the Holy anointment in the sacrament of the Holy Myron (Chrism) so that the Spirit may always work in him.

The Spirit may also work in the unbelievers for the benefit of the church.

As the Scriptures say, "*The Lord stirred up the spirit of Cyrus, King of Persia. (Ezra 1:1).* This was for the purpose of building the house of the Lord in Jerusalem. There are many similar events both in Scriptures and in history.

(8)

WHEN DID THE DISCIPLES RECEIVE THE HOLY SPIRIT?

Question:

When did the disciples receive the Holy Spirit? Was it when the Spirit came upon them in the form of tongues as of fire (Acts 2)? Or when the Lord breathed on them and said to them, *"Receive the Holy Spirit" (John 20)?*

Answer:

They received the Holy Spirit for permanent dwelling on the day of Pentecost.

At that time the Lord's promise was fulfilled that they would be, *"Endued with power from on high." (Luke 24:49)* and also the promise, *"If I do not go away, the Helper will not come to you: but if I depart, I will send Him to you." (John 16:7).* This text shows that they were to receive the Holy Spirit after the Lord's ascension to heaven which happened on the day of Pentecost (Acts 2:2-4).

But when the Lord breathed on them it was to give them the sacrament of the Holy Orders (Priesthood).

It is stated, "*He breathed on them and said to them 'Receive the Holy Spirit. If you forgive the sins of any, they are forgiven them, if you retain the sins of any, they are retained'*" *(John 20:22, 23).*

It means that He gave them, by the Holy Spirit, the authority to forgive sins, or rather He gave them the Spirit by whom they can forgive sins, thus forgiveness comes from God.

This breathe that gave the Holy Spirit is confined to them, not for all believers.

It is given to those who were to perform the work of priesthood from among the 'apostles' disciples and successors, whereas the coming of the Holy Spirit on the day of Pentecost was for all and the apostles gave this gift to people by the laying on of hands (Acts 8:17), then by the Holy anointment (1 John 2:20, 27) which is now given in the sacrament of Holy Chrism (Myron) to all believers.

Hence, the apostles received priesthood when the Lord breathed on them.

Then they took over this priesthood on the day of Pentecost when they baptised people.

The Lord knew that they were in need of Holy priesthood in order that they might baptise the new members of the church, loose and bind, and practise all other sacraments.

Therefore, He gave them the Holy Spirit - who was to give them priesthood - before giving them the Holy Spirit to dwell permanently in them as necessary for their ministry and lives as well.

(9)

IS THERE A GOSPEL OF ST. PAUL THE APOSTLE?

Question:

St. Paul the Apostle said, *"But I make known to you, brethren, that the gospel which was preached by me is not according to man..... but it came through the revelation of Jesus Christ." (Gal 1:11, 12).*

Is there a gospel of St. Paul?

Answer:

The word "gospel" is a Greek word meaning good news.

St. Paul the Apostle used it in this sense, not meaning a certain book. In some instances he said, *"The gospel of your salvation." (Eph 1:3),* i.e. the good news of your salvation. In other instances he said, *"The gospel of peace." (Eph 6:15)* meaning the good news of peace or preaching peace and *"The gospel of the glory of Christ." (2 Cor 4:4)* and *"The glorious gospel of the Blessed God." (1 Tim 1:11)* by which he means preaching about this glory.

Of course, there were no gospels carrying these or other names.

When St. Paul the Apostle said, *"The gospel for the uncircumcised had been committed to me, as the gospel for the circumcised was to Peter." (Gal 2:7),* he meant that he was entrusted to carry the gospel or the good news to the uncircumcised, i.e. the Gentiles and St. Peter to carry the gospel to the circumcised, i.e. to the Jews.

What is meant by gospel is the good news of salvation and redemption. He did not mean of course that there was a gospel called gospel for the uncircumcised and another called gospel for the circumcised.

The same is understood from all other words of the Apostle.

By the words, *"My chains for the gospel," (Philem 13),* he meant the imprisonment he undergoes for his preaching the gospel. And when he said, *"The things which happened to me have actually turned out for the furtherance of the gospel." (Philem 1:12),* he meant the furtherance of the preaching of salvation. By the words, *"I have begotten you through the gospel." (1 Cor 4:15),* he meant the preaching he preached. The same goes for all other texts because there were no written gospels at that time.

The Lord Christ Himself used the same expression.

At the beginning of His preaching - when John the Baptist was in prison - the Lord Christ came "preaching the gospel of the Kingdom of God and saying, *'The time is fulfilled and the Kingdom of God is at hand. Repent and believe in the gospel'" (Mark 1:14, 15)*.

Which gospel was it that the Lord Christ meant, though there were no written gospels at that time and He had not yet chosen His disciples?

He meant then to say "Believe in this preaching of the Kingdom which I preach you now."

It is the joyful news that the Kingdom of God is at hand.

Christianity came preaching salvation; salvation from the punishment of sin and of the dominion of the devil, eternal salvation through redemption. This preaching was given the name "gospel".

The same can be traced in the Lord Christ's words where He used the term "gospel" often.
An example of this is found in the words of the Lord to His disciples, **"*go into all the world and preach the gospel to every creature." (Mark 16:15)*.**

There was no written gospel at that time, but the Lord Christ meant preaching the news of salvation to all people.

The same applies to St. Paul the Apostle; by the words, "The gospel which was preached by me," he meant the good news of salvation which he preached.

Moreover, *"I went up again to Jerusalem..... and communicated to them the gospel which I preach among the Gentiles" (Gal 2:1, 2);* by which words he meant the preaching among the Gentiles that they also have attained salvation.

When he said, *"For God is my witness, Whom I serve with my spirit in the gospel of His Son" (Rom 1:9),* he meant preaching about His Son; for there is nothing called "the gospel of His Son" or "the gospel of Christ".

(10)

WHAT IS THE DIFFERENCE BETWEEN CHRIST AS SON OF GOD AND US AS CHILDREN OF GOD?

Question:

We are God's children and we pray, "Our Father Who are in heaven" and Christ is the Son of God; what is the difference between Christ's sonship to God and ours?

Answer:

The Lord Christ is the Son of God, of God's essence and same Divine Nature.

He is of the same divinity with all divine attributes. Hence He could say, *"He who has seen Me has seen the Father." (John 14:9)* and *"I and My Father are One." (John 10:30).* The Jews took up stones to stone Him because being a man, He made Himself God (John 10:31, 33). This fact was asserted by St. John the Evangelist when he said, *"The Word was God" (John 1:1).*

The Lord Christ is the Son of God since eternity, before the ages.

He is born of the Father before all ages as He said in His soliloquy with the Father, *"O Father, glorify Me together with Yourself with the glory which I had with You before the world was." (John 17:5).*

As He was before the world and being God's uttered reason it was said, *"All things were made through Him and without Him nothing was made that was made." (John 1:3).*

On the other hand, our sonship to God is a kind of adoption and honour granted in a certain time.

St. John the Beloved said, *"Behold what manner of love the Father has bestowed on us, that we should be called children of God!" (1 John 3:1).* We are called so, out of God's love for us. It was also said, *"But as many as received Him, to them He gave the right to become children of God, to those who believe in His name:" (John 1:12).*

Therefore, it is not natural sonship of His essence, otherwise we would be gods!! It is also connected with time, for it was not there before our believing and accepting baptism.

Since Christ's sonship to the Father is natural sonship of the same essence, He is called "The Only Begotten Son."

That is the Only Son of His essence, nature and divinity.

It was thus said, *"For God so loved the world that He gave His Only Begotten Son." (John 3:16)*.

The same expression - The Only Begotten Son - was repeated in (John 3:18) and in (John 1:18), *"No one has seen God at any time. The Only Begotten Son, who is in the bosom of the Father, He has declared Him,"* and also in (1 John 4:9), *"In this the love of God was manifested towards us, that God has sent His Only Begotten Son into the world, that we might live through Him."*

In being the Only Son, His sonship is certainly different from ours.

Therefore, this matchless sonship is received by us with belief and worship.

In the story of the man born blind, for example, when the Lord found the man who was cast out by the Jews, He said to him, *"Do you believe in the Son of God?"* and the man answered, *"Who is He, Lord, that I may believe in Him?"* and having known Him, the man said, *"Lord, I believe!"* and worshipped Him (John 9:35-38). If the Lord was just son of God like others, there would be no need for belief and worship.

Furthermore, believing in this sonship was the aim of the gospel.

St. John almost, at the end of the gospel, says *"And truly Jesus did many other signs in the presence of His disciples, which are not written in this book; but these are written that you may believe that Jesus is the Christ, the Son of GOD, and that*

believing you may have life in His name." (John 20:30, 31).
When St. Peter confessed this belief, saying, *"You are the Christ, the Son of the living God,"* the Lord considered his confession the rock on which the church was to be built *(Matt 16:16, 18).*

The Lord Christ, being alone the natural Son of the Father, was called the Son as in many verses demonstrating His Divinity.

The mere words "The Son" are taken to refer to the Lord Christ.

Some examples are:

+ *"For as the Father raises the dead and gives life to them, even so the Son gives life to whom He will. For the Father judges no one, but has committed all judgement to the Son, that all should honour the Son just as they honour the Father." (John 5:21-23).*

+ *"Therefore if the Son makes you free, you shall be free indeed." (John 8:36).*

+ *"He who believes in the Son has everlasting life; and he who does not believe the Son shall not see life, but the wrath of God abides on him." (John 3:36)*

+ *"Who makes His angels spirits and His ministers a flame of fire. But to the Son He says, 'Your Throne, O God, is forever and ever...'" (Heb 1:7, 8).*

There are many other examples which imply the same meaning.

Being the Son, He is worshipped by all God's angels.

About the greatness of the Lord Christ, the apostle said, *"But when He again brings the firstborn into the world, He says, 'Let all the angels of God worship Him'". (Heb 1:6).*

The Lord Christ was referred to as the Son of God on occasions of miracles.

+ When the centurion and those with him, who were guarding Jesus, saw the earthquake and the things that had happened, they feared greatly, saying, *"Truly this was the Son of God!" (Matt 27:54).*

+ Nathanael, when the Lord told him that he saw him under the fig tree, believed and said, *"Rabbi, You are the Son of God! You are the King of Israel!" (John 1:49).*

+ Those who were in the boat and saw him walking on the sea, came and worshipped him, saying, *"Truly you are the Son of God." (Matt 14:33).*

+ When the Lord Christ said to Martha before raising her brother, *"I am the resurrection and the life. He who believes in Me, though he may die, he shall live."* Martha answered, *"Yes, Lord, I believe that you are the Christ, the Son of God, who is to come into the world." (John 11:27).*

The testimony of John the Baptist at the time of the Lord's baptism with the accompanying wonders. St. John said, *"And I have seen and testified that this is the Son of God" (John 1:34).*

Therfore, it is evident that the Lord's sonship to the Father is not an ordinary sonship like that of all believers.

(11)

ADAM AND THE LORD CHRIST

Question:

I heard someone say that Adam is greater than Christ; for if Christ was born of a woman having no intercourse with a man, Adam was not born of a man nor of a woman? What is your opinion? Who is greater then?

Answer:

There is no ground at all for comparison between Adam and the Lord Christ. However, we shall state the following points:

1. The Lord Christ was born in a miraculous way indeed. No one ever has been or will ever be born in such a way. Adam, on the other hand, has nothing to do with birth; for he was created from the dust of the ground which is a lower case. As he was born of the dust of the ground he was called Adam, whereas the Lord Christ is born not created.

2. The Lord Christ is the Word of God (John 1:1), but Adam is just a servant of God.

3. The Lord Christ is distinguished from Adam by holiness and perfection.

Adam sinned and drew with him all the world to sin, but the Lord Christ is the only One who never sinned and is so called Holy (Luke 1:35). He is the only One who defied His generation, saying, *"Which of you convicts Me of sin?"*
(John 8:46).

4. Adam - because of his sin - was driven out of Paradise (the Garden). But the Lord Christ came to save Adam and his offspring and bring them again to Paradise. Is it reasonable then that he who was driven out of Paradise be greater than Him who brought him back to it?

5. Adam died and turned into dust after being eaten by worms and no one knows where he was buried. But the Lord Christ saw no corruption in His body. No one ever said that His body was eaten by worms, for He ascended to heaven and sat on the right hand of the Father.

6. Adam did not rise from the dead up till now and still waits the general resurrection, whereas the Lord Christ did rise in great glory and He will come at the end of ages for judgement, to judge the quick and the dead.

7. We never heard that Adam had a message to the world nor even had a history except that he was created, he sinned, he was driven out of Paradise and died and one of his sons was the first murderer in the world. But the Lord Christ had a great message; that of Salvation. He carried the sins of the whole world and died to redeem them. He rectified the errors of His generation and guided the people of His time, whereas Adam never did anything like this.

8. The Lord Christ was the Master and Teacher; He left the greatest doctrines to His generation and to all generations. All who heard Him were astonished at His nderstanding (Luke 2:47). But our father Adam left us nothing, not even a word or a piece of advice!

9. The Lord Christ worked miracles which no one ever worked, such as raising the dead, creating and wonderful healing miracles like that of healing the man born blind (John 9). We never heard that our father Adam worked a single miracle! Can we then compare him to the Lord Christ of Whom St. John the Beloved said that He had done many other miracles if written one by one, even the world itself could not contain the books that would be written (John 21:25).

10. The Lord Christ possessed the attributes of leadership, so He was followed by thousands; whereas Adam did not lead anyone, not even his wife but was rather led by her when she gave him of the prohibited fruit and he ate, contravening the commandment.

11. All the aforementioned is related to the human aspect, but with respect to the divinity of the Lord Christ, we cannot compare a person created to Him Who, "*All things were made through Him and without Him nothing was made that was made.*" *(John 1:3)*. This single point needs a whole book on Christ's Divinity.

12. It is true that Adam is the father of all of us, but to say that he is greater than the Lord Christ is unreasonable and unacceptable. Many of Adam's offspring were greater than him! And this has nothing to do with the respect due to him being a father.

(12)

WHY - AFTER SALVATION - DO MEN TOIL AND WOMEN CONCEIVE IN PAIN?

Question:

God inflicted punishment on Adam, "In the sweat of your face you shall eat bread", *"Cursed is the ground for your sake, in toil you shall eat of it." (Gen 3:19,17)* and He punished Eve, *"I will greatly multiply your sorrow and your conception; in pain you shaft bring forth children." (Gen 3:16).*

Then the Lord Christ came and saved us with His blood. Why then - after such salvation - there is a punishment still: Man toils to eat bread and woman in pain brings forth children?

Answer:

In fact the punishment of sin was death and the Lord Christ came to save us from death by dying on our behalf.

God's commandment to our father Adam was: *of the tree of the knowledge of good and evil you shall not eat, for in the day that you eat of it you shall surely die." (Gen 2:17)*.

Eve understood this well and mentioned it to the serpent, saying, *"...of the fruit of the tree which is in the midst of the Garden, God has said, 'You shall not eat it, nor shall you touch it, lest you die'". (Gen 3:3)*.

This is the teaching of the Holy Bible, for the apostle says, ***"For the wages of sin is death." (Rom 6:23)***. And about this death, he said also, *"And you...who were dead in trespasses and sins." (Eph 2:1)*. *"Even when we were dead in trespasses, made us alive together with Christ." (Eph 2:5; Col 2:13)*.

Since the wages of sin is death, the only way leading to salvation is redemption, by which one dies on behalf of another. This was the essential idea implied in the sacrifices of the Old Testament and the essence of the crucifixion and death of Christ for us. That is why we say that the Lord Christ bore our sins on the cross and died for them.

As for toil and pains of conception, they are temporal punishments.

They are not the original punishment, but just to remind us that we sinned and thus redemption be valuable in our eyes. Therefore God kept these punishments for our benefit to remind us. But some might not suffer these punishments - such as children for example- but they remember them when they grow up.

(13)

WHY DID WE NOT DIE IMMEDIATELY AFTER SINNING?

Question:

The Lord God said to our father Adam, "*But of the tree of the knowledge of good and evil you shall not eat, for in the day that you eat of it you shall surely die.*" *(Gen 2:17).*
Why then did not Adam and Eve die on the same day they ate of the tree?

Answer:

It seems that the question concentrates on the death of the body alone, whereas there are other kinds of deaths which our forefathers died on that same day:

1. There is moral death, by which our forefathers lost the divine image they had in the likeness of God (Gen 1:26, 27). After Adam had sinned, God said to him, "*Dust you are and to dust you shall return.*" *(Gen 3:19).* Thus, Adam became dust

after having been in God's image. This moral death appears also in Adam's being sent out of the Garden of Eden (Gen 3:23). As a consequence of this moral death, Adam lost the purity and innocence he had before eating of the tree and he got the knowledge of evil and became aware that he was naked (Gen 3:21).

2. **There is also spiritual death, which is separation from God.**

Adam became afraid from God and began to hide from His face and stand before Him as guilty and sinful. Sin is indeed death as the father said about his lost son, *"For this my son was dead." (Luke 5:24)*. The apostle also described the widow who lives in pleasure as dead while she lives (1 Tim 5:6). When Adam fell in sin, he deserved the description given afterwards to the Angel of the Church in Sardis, *"You have a name that you are alive but you are dead." (Rev 3:1)*. It was not the death of the body but spiritual death as that by which the widow who lives in pleasure was described.

3. **Adam and Eve were also under sentence of eternal death.**

That was the reason for being prevented by God from eating from the tree of life (Gen 3:22).

When he died, he went to Hades and waited for the salvation of Christ.

4. As for the death of the body, it began to work in Adam and his nature became mortal.

His nature became mortal from the moment he ate from the tree as we say in the Holy Mass, "The death that entered into the world by the envy of Satan."

However, this death delayed for the following reasons:

+ If Adam had died at that same moment, all of humanity would have perished and have no existence. We would have not been born, nor he who asked this question. But God had blessed Adam and Eve and said to them, "*Be fruitful and multiply; fill the earth and subdue it.*" *(Gen 1:28)*.

+ The blessing of multiple offspring must have come true because God is faithful even if we are faithless.

+ The coming of this offspring would give a chance for the coming of the Virgin from the offspring of Adam and Eve and the coming of the Lord Christ born from Her by whom salvation will be given and in whom all the nations of the earth shall be blessed (Gen 3:15, 22:18).

Postponing death was then necessary that the Lord Christ may come and effect salvation.

However, this postponement does not mean that the sentence of death was not executed fully and at that same time as aforementioned.

(14)

WHY DO WE DIE THOUGH SALVATION HAS BEEN EFFECTED?

Question:

Since the wages of sin is death and the Lord Christ died on our behalf and saved us, why then do we die?

Answer:

The Lord Christ saved us from spiritual and moral death.

With regard to spiritual death which is separation from God, the apostle tells us, *"We were reconciled to God through the death of His Son." (Rom 5:10)*.

As for moral death, the Lord delivered us from it restoring us to our first rank. He gave us again the divine image and as the apostle says about baptism, *"For as many of you as were baptised into Christ have put on Christ." (Gal 3:27)*.

We restored our moral position as God's children (1 John 3:1) and temples of His Holy Spirit (1 Cor 6:19).

He saved us from eternal death.

It is thus written in the Holy Bible, *"For God so loved the world that He gave His Only Begotten Son, that whoever believes in Him should not perish but have everlasting life." (John 3:16).*

Hence, the death of Christ for us gave us eternal life and by His death He saved us from eternal death. This is the basis of our salvation.

As for bodily death, it is no more death in fact. By bodily death we mean separation of the spirit from the body. Thus we say to the Lord in the Litany of the Departed, "It is not death of Your servants but rather transmission." It is transmission to Paradise and to communion with the Lord Christ. Therefore St. Paul the Apostle desired this death, saying, "... *having a desire to depart and be with Christ, which is far better." (Philem. 1:23).*

As St. Paul called it departure, so also Simeon the Elder called it. He prayed to God, saying, *"Lord, now You are letting Your servant depart in peace, according to Your word; for my eyes have seen Your salvation." (Luke 2:29, 30).*

Each of these two saints : Paul and Simeon the Elder desired this (death), for each saw in it release from the prison of the flesh and St. Paul considered it far better than this life.

Hence, bodily death is not considered punishment.

It is just a golden bridge leading us to the happy eternity. Moreover, this so called death does great favour to us; for without it we shall remain in this corruptible nature of the flesh, whereas through it we shall attain a more sublime nature.

It is the way to put off corruption and put on incorruption.

God, the lover of mankind, does not want us to remain in this nature which became corrupt with sin, this corruptible nature which is subject to hunger, thirst, fatigue and illness and which can do wrong. He, in his love, wills to transfer us from such nature to a better condition of which the apostle said in *(1 Cor 15:49),* **"As we have borne the Image of the man of dust, we shall also bear the image of the heavenly."**

He then explains in more detail, *"For this corruptible must put on incorruption; and this mortal must put on immortality." (1 Cor 15:53).*

The apostle says also, *"The body is sown in corruption, it is raised in incorruption. It is sown in dishonour, it is raised in glory. It is sown in weakness, it is raised in power. It is sown a natural body, it is raised a spiritual body." (1 Cor 15:42-44).*

Death, then, is the natural way that leads us to the glories of the Resurrection.

If we continue in the present nature - without death - we would sustain great loss. Thus, it is not right to consider death as punishment, but rather as change into a better nature.

Suppose that God abolished this bodily death as a result of salvation, what can be expected as a consequence?

Do you think that remaining in this material body of dust is the optimum status for man?

Remember that this includes what accompanies the old age, whether weakness or sickness. Moreover the complaint of those around, as the poet said what means that a person hopes to live though long life may be harmful to him. He will lose his cheerfulness and finds pain after comfort. His days might betray him and he will find nothing pleasant.

The optimum condition for man is the bright spiritual body which rises in power, in glory and in incorruption and this is what God wanted for us by death.

The question might have been serious if there was no resurrection after death in such glory.

It is the resurrection that will deliver us from the bondage of corruption, for which the whole creation groans and labours with birth pangs eagerly waiting for this redemption of our body (Rom 8:21-23).

(15)

OUR ATTITUDE TOWARDS THE LORD CHRIST'S BLOOD.

Question:

Someone said to me, since the Blood of the Lord Christ is for all people and he has forgiven all, even the atheist and wicked, we should then be confident of the sufficiency of His Blood no matter what might be our condition. Our attitude towards the Lord Christ is not important, but His attitude towards us! What is your opinion of these words?

Answer:

It is true that the Blood of Christ is for all people and we should be confident of the sufficiency of His Blood: for He gave us redemption sufficient for the forgiveness of the sins of all people in all generations, but.....**the words "Our attitude towards the Lord Christ is not important" are completely wrong and against the teaching of the Lord Himself.**

First, a person must believe in the Lord Christ and His Blood and must accept Christ and His redemption; for, no doubt, he who does not believe will be condemned (Mark 16:16). Do not say then that our attitude towards Christ is not important, because if we do not believe in the Lord Christ and the efficacy of His Blood, we cannot attain redemption or forgiveness.

Though the Blood of Christ is for all people and the salvation of Christ is for all, yet, none but those who believe in him will attain this salvation. This fact is indicated by the Holy Bible,

"Whoever believes in Him should not perish." (John 3:16).

He did not say "all the world" but "whoever believes in Him."

Therefore the words "He has forgiven all, even the atheist and wicked" cannot be accepted as long as the atheist remains atheist and the wicked remains wicked.

There is no forgiveness for the atheist unless they forsake atheism and believe in the Lord Christ.

This is an attitude which they should have towards Christ. They should believe and accept the Lord Christ bearing their sins and saving them. Without accepting Christ, they will not attain forgiveness as it is stated in the Holy Bible, *"But as many as received Him, to them He gave the right to become children of God." (John 1:12).*

The Lord Christ's attitude towards you is clear, what about your attitude towards him?

He wants to save you, but He will not do this without you.

He is standing at the door knocking, but you must open the door.

He says to you, *"Behold, I stand at the door and knock. If anyone hears My voice and opens the door, I will come into him and dine with him and he with Me." (Rev 3:20).*

So, if you do not open - this shows your attitude towards Him - you will not attain salvation. How easy it is for Him to leave you to your obstinacy until you cry out, *"My beloved had turned away and was gone..... I sought him, but I could not find him." (Song 5:6).*

Do not say then that our attitude is not important, but His!

If the matter depends on the Lord Christ wholly all people would be saved.

"He desires all men to be saved and to come to the knowledge of truth." (1 Tim 2:4).

However, there should be a human response, otherwise the Lord will say, as He said before to Jerusalem, *"How often I wanted..... but you were not willing! See! your house is left to you desolate." (Matt 23:37, 38).*

How can it be that one's attitude be not important? See what the Lord Christ says, **"*But whoever denies Me before men, him I will also deny before My Father Who is in heaven.*" *(Matt 10:33).*** This is due to one's attitude.

Accepting the Lord Christ, believing in Him and in His redemption are essential matters and principal attitude that a person should take instead of being passive towards Christ....

What else?

The Lord says, "*He who believes and is baptised will be saved.*" *(Mark 16:16).*

It is not sufficient only to believe so that you may attain the deserts of the Lord Christ's Blood, but you should also get baptised. You should be, "*Buried with Him through baptism.*" *(Rom 6:3)*, to die with Him and arise with Him. That is why Ananias said to Saul of Tarsus - after he accepted the Lord and believed in Him - "*Brother Saul ... why are you waiting? Arise and be baptised and wash away your sins.*" *(Acts 22:13, 16).*

Can you say then "Why should I be baptised, what avails is the attitude of Christ towards me?" By being baptised, you put on Christ, as St. Paul said, "*For as many of you as were baptised into Christ have put on Christ.*" *(Gal 3:27).*

Among other serious things regarding your attitude is the Holy Communion for example:

The Lord says, "*Unless you eat the Flesh of the Son of Man and drink His Blood, you have no life in you...He who eats My Flesh and drinks My Blood abides in Me and I in him.*" *(John 6:53, 56).*

Would you say then "I will not eat His Flesh nor drink His Blood. What is important is His attitude towards me!"

Do you think that life with God is a passive attitude on your part?

Do you want God to do everything and you remain passive, as if you were led unto doing good or were not participating with God in work?

What then would be the difference between the righteous and the wicked? The Lord Christ says, "*Whoever does the will of My Father in heaven is My brother and sister and mother.*" *(Matt 12:50).*

Hence, you must decide your attitude towards Him by doing His will.

Or do you want to be among God's people without doing His will and are satisfied with His attitude towards you? See what the Holy Bible says, "*Every tree which does not bear good fruit is cut down and thrown into the fire.*" *(Matt 3:10).* Now are you bearing fruit, or you are satisfied with the attitude of Him who willed and implanted you in His vineyard?

His attitude is to implant you in His vineyard and your attitude is to bear fruit.

He ever requires this from us, saying, "*Abide in My love. If you keep My commandments, you will abide in My love.*" *(John 15:9, 10)*.

You should take an attitude towards the Lord Christ, you should love Him as He loved you so that love may not be from one part only, the part of Christ who loved you and sacrificed His Blood for you.

If you do love Him, do not sin against Him and if you had lived before in sin, you should decide your attitude now by repenting.

Repentance is essential as an attitude on your part so that you may benefit from the Blood of the Lord Christ.

The Lord Himself says, "*Unless you repent, you will all likewise perish,*" *(Luke 13:3)*.

Would you not then repent, but say "What avails is Christ's attitude towards me?"

The foregoing words represent the Lord Christ's attitude towards those who do not repent: they will perish.

His attitude towards you is that He wants to wipe out your sins with His Blood, provided that you repent, otherwise you will not benefit from the Lord Christ's Blood.

Does the sinner have a share in the Blood of Christ?

Yes, provided that he repents. His attitude is thus important.

(16)

HOW CAN HE DIE THOUGH HE IS GOD?

Question:

Is it possible that Christ dies though He is God? Can God die? Was the death of Christ a weakness? Who was managing the world during His death?

Answer:

God cannot die. The divinity cannot undergo death.

Thus, we say in the Trisagion, "Holy is God, Holy is the Powerful, Holy is the Living and Immortal."

However, the Lord Christ is not only Godhead, but He is united with a human body.

He took on Himself a body of our human nature and that is why He was called "Son of Man". His human body is united with a human spirit which is mortal like ours, but it is united with the divine nature without separation.

When He died on the cross, He died in the body; in the human body.

Thus, we say in the ninth hour prayer, "You who tasted death in the body at the ninth hour...."

The death of Christ was not out of weakness, nor was it against His divinity.

It was not against His divinity because the Godhead is living - by His nature - and is immortal.

Moreover, He willed that His human body dies as a pleasing sacrifice and also for the redemption of the world.

His death was not also out of weakness for the following reasons:

1. His death was not weakness, but rather love and sacrifice as the Holy Bible says, *"No one has greater love than this, to lay down one's life for one's friends." (John 15:13).*

2. The Lord Christ offered Himself to death by His own will. He laid down His life to redeem humanity from the judgement of death. This is evident in His great words, "I lay down My life that I may take it again. *"No one takes it from Me, but I lay it down of Myself. I have power to lay it down, and I have power to take it again. This command I have received from My Father." (John 10:17, 18).*

The weakness of an ordinary person in his death lies in two matters:

a) An ordinary person dies against his will and he has no power to escape from death, unlike the Lord Christ who laid down His life without anyone taking it from Him.

b) When an ordinary person dies, he cannot rise unless God raises him. But the Lord Christ has risen by Himself and said about His life, "I have power to take it up again." These words can only be said by one who is powerful not weak.

3. Among the signs of the Lord's power in His death are the following:

a) In His crucifixion and death, "At that moment the curtain of the temple was torn in two, from top to bottom and the earth quaked, and the rocks were split, and the graves were opened; and many bodies of the saints who had fallen asleep were raised " So when the centurion and those with him, who were guarding Jesus, saw the earthquake and the things that had happened, they feared greatly, saying, *"Truly this was the Son of God!"(Matt 27:51-54)*.

b) In His death He worked also; for He opened Paradise and let in Adam, the other righteous people and the thief.

c) Through His death He abolished death (2 Tim 1:10), (Heb 2:14). Thus death became a mere golden bridge bringing people to a better life. Therefore St. Paul the Apostle said, "*O Death, where is your sting?" (1 Cor 15:55).*

Who then administered the universe during His death?

It was His Godhead who administered the universe; His Godhead that never dies and was never affected by the death of the body. The Godhead is present everywhere and is also in heaven (John 3:13).

(17)

HOW DID THE LORD CHRIST DIE WHILE HIS DIVINITY WAS NOT SEPARATED FROM HIS HUMANITY?

Question:

How did the Lord die though we say that His divinity was not separated from His humanity even for a moment or a twinkle of an eye?

Answer:

The death of the Lord Christ means the separation of His spirit from His body, not the separation of His divinity from His humanity.

Death belongs to the body - to humanity alone. It is a separation between the two elements of humanity, i.e. the spirit and the body. This does not mean that divinity was separated from humanity.

The beautiful Syrian Fraction prayed in the Holy Mass explains this fact in clear words. It says:

"His spirit was separated from His body, but His divinity has never been separated from His spirit nor from His body."

The human spirit was separated from the human body, while the Godhead was not separated from any of them but remained united with them as before death. The only difference is that before death the Godhead was united with the spirit and the body of Christ together, whereas after death, the Godhead was united with them while each of them was apart from the other, i.e., the Godhead became united with the human spirit alone and with the human body alone.

A proof of this fact - i.e. the Godhead was united with the Lord's human spirit during His death - is that the Lord's spirit, being united with the Godhead, was able to open Paradise that had been closed since Adam's sin and could go to Hades and release the righteous people of the old times who departed in hope letting all of them into Paradise with the thief who was on the Lord's right hand on the cross and whom the Lord promised, *"Today you will be with Me in Paradise." (Luke 23:43)*.

The proof of the Godhead being united with the Lord's body during His death is that the body remained completely undecayed and He could rise on the third day and come out of the closed tomb in mystery and power; the power of the Resurrection.

What happened then in the Resurrection?

In the Resurrection the Lord Christ's human spirit united with the Godhead, was united with the body that was united with the Godhead also. The divinity never was separate from humanity neither before nor during death nor after it.

(18)

THE BODY OF THE LORD CHRIST IN THE CHURCH AND EUCHARIST.

Question:

Is it true that the body of the Lord Christ, i.e., the Church, is the same body on the altar and the same body that ascended into heaven and sat on the Father's right hand, both being One? Is this mentioned in the sayings of any of the father saints?

Answer:

1. The Lord's body that is on the altar is the body born by the Holy Virgin Mary, the body that was crucified, buried and risen, that ascended into heaven and sat on the right hand of the Father.

As for the Lord's body, meaning the Church, it refers to the whole congregation of believers and it is not reasonable to say that they all were born of the Holy Virgin.

Is it possible that the millions of Christians who live now, the millions who departed and the millions who will be born in future, all of them are born of the Holy Virgin as the body who sat on the Father's right hand and moreover they are that same body?

2. We worship the Lord's body that is on the altar and say, "We worship Your Holy Body, O Lord." We say also, "His divinity was not separated from His humanity not even for a moment or a twinkling of an eye." We say the same to the body that ascended and sat on the right hand of the Father.

It is different from the body of the Lord meaning the Church; for we do not worship the Church nor say about it - as a body - that its divinity was not separated from its humanity!!

3. The Lord Christ's body that is on the altar is the body that redeemed us and died for us then ascended into heaven in glory. Can we say then it is the church that redeemed us, died for us and ascended into heaven in glory?

4. We partake of the Lord's Body and Blood on the altar, do we partake of the Church (if we agree that the Church and the Lord's Body are One)? God forbid...

5. The Lord Christ's Body, meaning the Church, is not yet complete. There are
members that have not yet joined it, i.e., those who are not yet born and those who will accept faith in future.

But the Lord Christ's Body that is on the altar and in heaven is perfect without deficiency and no other members will join it.

6. The Lord Christ's Body, meaning the Church, is ourselves while His Body that is on the altar and in heaven is Christ Himself. If both are One, are we then Christ?
Are we sitting now on the Father's right hand? Are we in heaven? And when we partake do we partake of the Church or of Christ?

7. The Lord Christ's Body, meaning the Church, includes all the believers who have not yet completed their struggle and who are still struggling against the evil powers and not yet crowned. As for the Lord's body that is on the altar and sitting on the right hand of the Father, it has no members who are still struggling the evil power to conquer and be crowned. It has overcome and is glorified and helps us to walk in the procession of His victory.

8. The Lord Christ's body on the altar is a real body in the literal meaning of the word "body". But the Church is the Lord's Body in the spiritual meaning as it is His bride in the spiritual meaning also.......

9. If the Church is the same Body of the Lord Christ that is on the altar and on the Father's right, we would be lead to the heresy of "the one existence" in which many philosophers and heretics fell.

10. No one of the fathers adopted this wrong opinion and if it is attributed by any Christian writer to any saint, this writer is certainly wrong in conveying the words or in understanding the intent of the saint and should make sure of the text and its source.

It is impossible that any of the saints speak words contradicting faith exposing himself to criticism as we have seen while analysing this thought.

Dear reader, you should examine carefully all that you read and don't believe what some may attribute to saints which saints did not say.

(19)

SATURDAY & SUNDAY

Question:

A Sabbatherian Adventist priest visited us and said, "It is written in the Holy Bible, "Heaven and earth will pass away, but My words will not pass away" and the Law commands us to keep the Sabbath holy. Why then do we not keep it?"

Answer:

The Law commanded in the Old Testament keeping the Sabbath, but it also commanded to offer animal sacrifices for every sin and trespass (Lev 4), do this Adventist priest and his followers offer animal sacrifices in obedience to the Law?
Does he offer these sacrifices in the Temple in Jerusalem? Or he breaks the Law in this point. Does he keep the fasting of the fourth month, the fifth month, the seventh month and the tenth month as the Bible says in (Zech 8:19)? Does he celebrate the festival of booths, the festival of trumpets, the festival of the weeks and the festival of the unleavened bread as the Law commands in (Lev 23)? Why does not he say about these

festivals *"not one letter, not one stroke of a letter will pass from the Law until all is accomplished." (Matt 5:18)?*

Does he and his family celebrate the Passover every year and bring a lamb and keep it from the tenth to the fourteenth day, then they eat it roasted over the fire with unleavened bread and bitter herbs with their loins girded, sandals on their feet, staff in their hand and eat it hurriedly then for seven days they eat unleavened bread and remove leaven from their houses according to the Law (Ex 12:6-9). Is this Adventist priest descending from Aaron as the Law requires?

Does he keep the commandments of the Law as stipulated in the Old Testament? Does he observe all rules of uncleanliness and purification and abstain from foods prohibited by the Law? **Or is it only the Sabbath that concerns him whereas** *"For whoever shall keep the whole law, and yet stumble in one point, he is guilty of all." (Jas 2:10).*

Would that this Adventist brother come out of the letter to the spirit and oversteps the symbol to the thing symbolised; for some commandments are given to us in the Old Testament in order that we understand it in a new spiritual way in the New Testament. Would that he listens to the words of the apostle, " if you died with Christ from the basic principles of the world, why, as though living in the world, do you subject yourselves to regulations; *"Do not touch, do not taste, do not handle " (Col 2:20, 21).*

Such commandments are only "a shadow of what is to come" including also the commandment of the Sabbath. So, the apostle says,"*So let no one judge you in food or in drink, or regarding a festival or a new moon or sabbaths* ". *(Col 2:16)*.

So, the commandment of the Sabbath - in its literal meaning - ended and let no one condemn you for it as the apostle said about the Sabbath and other regulations which are, "*a shadow of things to come,.*" *(Col 2:17)*.

And so long as the Holy Bible considered the Sabbath one of the regulations which are a shadow of what is to come, which means that it was a mere symbol and changed by the appearance of the thing symbolised ie. Sunday, thus we are not requested to keep it literally according to this express commandment of the New Testament.

However, God's words do not pass away; the Sabbath, in its spiritual meaning, is still kept. What then is its spiritual meaning?

The word "Sabbath" means rest and the commandment of keeping this weekly rest for the Lord is still existing; for we take rest in the real Lord's Day which is Sunday, on which the Lord took rest actually. What does this mean? How did the Lord take rest on Sunday?

The Lord took rest after offering His blood on Friday for our salvation by paying the debt of sin in full on the cross. He released all the world from the debt of sin, but death remained.

The Lord had to release us from death as well so as it does not continue as a ghost terrifying us and He released us from it on Sunday by His resurrection and victory over death. Thus Sunday became the real rest of the Lord on which He released us from death and from the wages of death.

Would that we take the spirit not the letter of the Law.

It is written, the letter kills, but the Spirit gives life. (2 Cor 3:6)

The spirit of the Law is the rest on the Lord's day and the great day of the Lord was Sunday on which He got rid of death which was the most dangerous enemy of man.

For more detail, see my book "The Ten Commandments - Part 1 - Fourth Commandment".

(20)

WHY DO WE BAPTISE BABES WHO HAVE NOT YET BELIEVED?

Question:

Since the Lord Christ has said, "*He who believes and is baptised will be saved.*" *(Mark 16:16),* **why then are children baptised before accepting faith?**

Answer:

We baptise children because baptism is necessary for their salvation.

The Lord Christ said to Nicodemus, "*Most assuredly, I say to you, unless one is born of water and the Spirit.*" *(John 3:5).*

We baptise children so that they become members of the church and benefit from Its spiritualities.

They benefit from the church Sacraments, they come to the church and take part in celebrating the Holy Mass and have communion.

Why do we deprive children of such spiritual atmosphere and benefits? Is it because they are young? The Lord Christ says, *"Let the little children come to Me, and do not forbid them; for of such is the kingdom of heaven " (Matt 19:14).*

Some may object saying that a child cannot accept faith and faith is necessary for salvation. We reply: **Faith is necessary for the grown ups who need to be convinced by reasoning.**

The grown up need preaching and ministry of the word to be convinced and accept faith, whereas children believe whatever we say to them. They have no objection to faith: for they have not attained yet the age of doubt and argument. On the other hand, the grown ups should declare their faith before baptism and should learn the rules of faith as the church used to do for the catechumens before their receiving baptism.

Children are baptised according to the faith of their parents.

In the Holy Bible, there are many examples of children who were baptised after the faith of their parents and joined the church as members (among the believers) on the basis of their parents' faith also. Among those are:

1. **Salvation of the firstborn by the blood of the Passover lamb.**

The symbol is very clear in this great historical event. The Passover is a symbol of the Lord Christ as St. Paul said, *"For indeed Christ, our Passover, was sacrificed for us." (1 Cor 5:7)* and the Passover blood is a symbol of the blood of Christ by which we attained salvation as the Lord said, *"When I see the blood, I will pass over you." (Ex 12:13)*.

Here we inquire: Had the children who were saved by the Passover blood believed in the blood first?

Of course not, but they were saved because of the faith of their parents who sprinkled the doors with the blood trusting the Lord's words and trusting that the blood will save their children from perdition and it happened.

Was it necessary to ask every child saved whether he had believed in the Passover blood first or not?

Perhaps some were still babes knowing nothing.

2. The Children who were saved from slavery of Pharaoh by crossing the Red Sea.

The symbol of salvation is very clear here. The crossing of the Red Sea was considered baptism by St. Paul the Apostle (1 Cor 10:2). Most of these children crossed the Sea on the shoulders of their parents not knowing what was going on.
But their parents believed in the Lord's promise of salvation to Moses and they crossed the Sea in trust. Their faith saved their children with them.

3. The Children who were circumcised on the eighth day:
Circumcision was a symbol of baptism, through which a child

becomes a member of God's people and unless a child is baptised he perishes. What did a child understand from all this? What was his belief on his eighth day from birth? Should we have asked such a child about his belief in the circumcision law as given by the Lord to our father Abraham (Gen 17). Was not he circumcised according to the faith of his parents and this was accounted righteousness for him and he joined God's people by it?

4. The children who were baptised among their families.

It is written about Lydia, the purple cloth dealer, that *"she and her household were baptised." (Acts 16:15)*. The children were not excluded. It is said also about the jailer who believed through the preaching of Paul and Silas, *"Immediately he and all his family were baptized." (Acts 16:33)*. Was there not any child among all those? The same is said about Crispus the official of the Synagogue (Acts 18:8). St. Paul the Apostle says also that he had baptised "the household of Stephanas." (1 Cor 1:16) without excluding the children.

In General, no verse in the Holy Bible prohibits baptising children.

However, when children grow up, their faith will be tested. If they were steadfast they will continue in their faith, if not they will not benefit as in the case of grown ups who were baptised but were not steadfast, no difference.

(21)

WHY DOES ONE SIN AFTER RENEWAL OF BAPTISIM?

Question:

Do we not believe that a person is renewed in baptism (Rom 6:4)? Why then does one sin after baptism in spite of being renewed?

Answer:

In baptism, one obtains renewal, not infallibility.

No one on earth is infallible. Notice David the prophet in the Old Testament: how the Spirit of the Lord came upon him (1 Sam 16:13) but this did not prevent him from sinning afterwards (2 Sam 24:10). Samson also, " *the Spirit of the LORD began to move upon him." (Judg 13:25)* " *And the Spirit of the LORD came mightily upon him." (Judg 14:6)*, however, he sinned and broke his vow (Judg 16:19, 20).

Thus, renewal in baptism does not mean that a person does not sin thereafter.

The principle is that one's nature becomes inclined to righteousness and sin becomes incidental.

This means that a person's spiritual capabilities become extensive and he becomes worthy to have the Holy Spirit dwell in him through the Holy Chrism (Myron). When he sins, his conscience blames him quickly and he becomes ready to return to God.

Not to sin at all will only be realised in eternity where we shall put on the crown of righteousness. St. Paul the Apostle said, *"Finally, there is laid up for me the crown of righteousness, which the Lord, the righteous Judge, will give to me on that Day, and not to me only but also to all who have loved His appearing." (2 Tim 4:8)* This means that our nature will be crowned with righteousness in the other life and will have righteousness as a nature so as not to sin afterwards. (See my book, "Life of Repentance and Purity" the Chapter on "Purity").

Here, on earth, the righteous fall seven times and rise again (Prov 24:16).

They are still considered righteous because righteousness is the principle, whereas falling is incidental. One falls and gets purified through repentance.

(22)

CAN A BLESSING BE TAKEN FROM A HUMAN?

Question:

If blessing belongs to God, can blessing be taken from a human? Can a person bless another person? What is the biblical evidence of this?

Answer:

Yes, a blessing can be taken from a human and in this case it will be a blessing from God Himself. There are many examples for this in the Holy Bible such as:

- **The blessing given by Isaac to Jacob.**

Isaac blessed his son Jacob (Gen 27) and Jacob became blessed from God and became favoured than Esau. He took the rights of the firstborn and priesthood and from his offspring Christ came and all the families of the earth are blessed in him and in his offspring (Gen 28:14). Esau wept for losing this right of the firstborn (Gen 27:38).

It is written also, *"By faith Isaac blessed Jacob and Esau concerning things to come." (Heb 11:20).*

Jacob, likewise, blessed his sons.

His blessing came true with respect to each one of his sons as if every word from him was coming from the mouth of God Himself. And when Jacob blessed Ephraim and Manasseh putting his right hand on Ephraim the younger and his left on Manasseh the elder, Ephraim became greater than Manasseh (Gen 48:13-20). *"So he blessed them that day, saying, 'By you Israel will invoke blessings, saying God make you like Ephraim and like Manasseh', So he put Ephraim before Manasseh."* And the blessing came true. Jacob blessed also Joseph his son (Gen 48:15, 49:22-26).

✣ **Preceding these, our father Noah blessed his sons and cursed Canaan.**

The sons of our father Noah whom he blessed became blessed and on the other hand Canaan whom Noah cursed (Gen 9:26, 27) became cursed even from the mouth of the Lord Christ in His talk with the Canaanite Woman (Matt 15:22, 26).
From all this, many blessings came: The blessing of the parents:

✣ **Whoever honours his parents is blessed**,

How much rather if those parents are holy people. An example of the blessing of the parents is that in *(Gen 31:55), "And early in the morning Laban arose, and kissed his sons and daughters and blessed them."*

✢ **The blessing of the righteous.**

The Holy Bible mentions this clearly as in: *(Prov 11:11)*, *"By the blessing of the upright a city is exalted."*

(Prov 28:20) "A faithful man will abound with blessings."

The men of God also blessed people as when Simon the elderly blessed the holy Virgin and Joseph the Carpenter (Luke 2:34).

✢ **The righteous person does not only bless others but he himself becomes a blessing.**

The Lord said to our father Abraham, *"I will make you a great nation; I will bless you And make your name great; And you shall be a blessing." (Gen 12:2).* And to the house of Judah the Lord said, *"I will save you, and you shall be a blessing." (Zech 8:13).*

Likewise, Elijah was a blessing to the house of the widow of Zarephath and Joseph the righteous to the house of Potiphar and to Egypt.

✢ **There is also the blessing of priesthood**:

There is the blessing of Moses the prophet & priest (Psa 99:6) to the people as it is written, *"Then Moses looked over all the work, and indeed they had done it; as the LORD had commanded, just so they had done it. And Moses blessed them." (Ex 39:43).* The Lord even explained the way by which Aaron's sons should bless people, He said to Moses, " Speak to Aaron and his sons, saying, 'This is the way you shall bless the children of Israel. Say to them: "The LORD bless you and keep you; The LORD make His face shine upon you, And be gracious to you; The LORD lift up His countenance upon you, And give you peace". (Num 6:22-26).

Another example of the blessing of priesthood is when Melchizedek the priest of God Most High blessed Abraham the Patriarch (Gen 14:19, Heb 7:1). St. Paul the Apostle explained that the inferior is blessed by the superior (Heb 7:7).

✥ **There is also the blessing of the prophets as men of God.**

We read about King Saul that he went out to seek the blessing of Samuel the Prophet (1 Sam 13:10).
Likewise, some leaders sent messengers to David seeking his blessing (1 Chr 18:10).

Solomon the Wise as well - having divine inspiration blessed all the people (1 Kin 8:14), *"Then the king turned around and blessed all the assembly of Israel". (2 Chr 6:3), "Then Solomon stood before the altar of the Lord in the presence of the all assembly of Israel and spread out his hands." (2 Chr 6:12).*

And Jehu the king blessed Jehonadab son of Rechab (2 Kin 10:15).

✥ **Another blessing is the blessing of the needy to those who give them charity.**

It is the blessing which a benevolent obtains from a person whom he offered help or saved from perdition. Job the Righteous said in this respect, *"The blessing of a perishing man came upon me." (Job 29:13).* It means that he took the blessing of the person whom he saved.

☦ There is a blessing which stands for prayer by anybody.

The apostle says, *"Bless those who persecute you; bless and do not curse them." (Rom 12:4).* And the Lord Christ says in the Sermon on the Mount, *"Pray (bless) for those who persecute you." (Matt 5:44).*

St. Peter as well says, *"not returning evil for evil or reviling for reviling, but on the contrary blessing, knowing that you were called to this, that you may inherit a blessing." (1 Pet 3:9).*

So, blessing can be given by one person to another to sum up all the above, we mention the following blessings given by humans:

1. Blessing of our forefathers.
2. Blessing of the parents.
3. Blessing of the righteous.
4. Blessing of the clergy.
5. Blessing of the prophets and anointed persons.
6. Blessing of the needy to those who give them charity.
7. Blessing by anybody as a prayer.

The blessing of those might be a prayer to which God responds and blesses. They are vessels in which blessing of God is conveyed. God entrusted them with His stores to
give from them to others...

(23)

THE HOLY TRINITY OF CHRISTIANITY AND THE SO CALLED TRINITY OF HEATHEN.

Question:

Is there any similarity between the Holy Trinity of Christianity and the pagan trinity? Or what is the difference? And was the cause of spreading Christianity in Egypt the similarity between the Trinity of Christianity and the pagan trinity as manifested in the story of Osoris, Isis and Horus?

Answer:

If we say that the cause of spreading Christianity quickly in Egypt is the similarity between its dogmas and the dogmas of the pharaonic Egypt, what then is the cause of the spreading of Christianity in other countries of the world?

Was it also a matter of similarity of dogmas? And if there was similarity, why was Christianity persecuted by paganism?

Why did the pagans kill St. Mark who preached the gospel in Egypt? Why had there been harsh conflict between paganism and Christianity along four centuries which ended with the extermination of paganism as its worshippers abandoned it and the idols were destroyed... !

No doubt Christianity revealed the falsehood and wrong concepts of paganism and not the similarity! Otherwise there would have been no need for a new religion to replace paganism.

As regards the dogma of the Trinity, it is clear that paganism does not believe in it.

Paganism believes in plurality of gods on a large scale not in trinity.

Pharaonic Egypt believed in god "Raa" who created god "Sho" and goddess "Neftoot." These two married and gave birth to god "Gab" the god of earth and goddess "Nout" goddess of heaven.

These in turn married and gave birth to Osoriso, Isis, Sett and Naftis. "Osoris" & "Isis" married and begot god Horus. There were also many other gods worshipped by the Egyptians.

Where then is the trinity amidst all this multitude of gods?

Can we choose three of those gods and call them trinity?

In the story of Osoris and Isis for example, we mentioned ten Egyptian gods. Even in this story when Isis saved her murdered husband Osoris and restored him to life, she was helped by Tohoot, god of wisdom, Anobis, god of mummification and by her sister Naftis. It is not then confined to a trinity i.e. to three gods and the old Egyptian dogmas have no such dogma known as trinity.

However, we say:

Christianity does not only believe in trinity but in Trinity and Oneness (monotheism).

This monotheism is not acceptable to the old religions which believe in plurality.

The Christian Creed begins with "Truly we believe in One God", and after in the name of the Father, the Son and the Holy Spirit, we say, "One God. Amen". And St. John the Evangelist says in his first epistle, *"For there are three that bear witness in heaven: the Father, the Word, and the Holy Spirit; and these three are one." (1 John 5:7).*

The Words "God is one" are stated in many places of the Holy Bible:

It is mentioned in (Gal 3:20), in (Jas 2:19), in (Eph 4:5), in (1 Tim 2:5), in (John 5:44), in (Rom 3:30), in (Matt 19:17) and in (Mark 12:29, 32). It also represented the first Commandment (Ex 20:3), how clear was the text of that commandment *"The LORD our God, the LORD is one!" (Deut 6:4).*

This same phrase "One God" was mentioned many times in Isaiah on the mouth of God Himself as in (Is 43:10, 11), (Is 45:6, 18, 21), (Is 46:9).

Christianity proclaims that the three persons (Hypostases) are One God.

This is stated in (1John 5:7) and in the words of the Lord Christ *".... baptising them in the name of the Father and of the Son and of the Holy Spirit." (Matt 28:19). He said "in the name" not "in the names".*

Perhaps one may ask how $1+1+1 = 1$, we reply that $1 \times 1 \times 1 = 1$.

The Trinity represents the One God with His wisdom and His Spirit, as we say of a person that he and his mind and spirit are one being and that the fire with its light and heat are one thing.

Osoris, Isis and Horus on the other hand are not one but three gods.

This is the first difference between this story and the Holy Trinity of Christianity.

The second difference lies in the story of a marriage between a man god, Osoris and a woman goddess, Isis, begetting a son god, Horus.

There is no women nor marriage in the Christianity, God forbids!

If we say that every father, mother & son from a trinity, it would be in every place, in every country and in every family. However, this has nothing to do with the Christian Trinity.

The Son in Christianity is not the offspring of a sexual propagation.

God forbids that this be in Christianity, for God is Spirit (John 4:24) and He is above sexual propagation. The Son in Christianity is God's uttered wisdom or God's wise utterance. The Son's filiation to the Father in the Trinity is the same as we say the mind begets a thought, yet the mind and the thought is one thing without sexual propagation.

A thought comes out of the mind while still in it and not separate from it, whereas in sexual propagation, the son has an independent entity separate from his father and mother who each has a separate independent entity as well. That is the difference between this and the Christian Trinity.

The Persons of the Christian Trinity are not separate from each other.

The Son says *"I am in the Father and the Father is in Me." (John 14:11).* *"I and My Father are One." (John 10:30).* Horus cannot say I and Osoris are one! He is in me and I am in him.

Furthermore the Persons of the Christian Trinity are equal in being eternal not differing in time.

God has His wisdom and Spirit since eternity.

But in the story of Osoris and Isis the son Horus was not in existence before being born, he came to existence afterwards. There may also be some difference in age between Osoris and Isis and they also came to existence only when being born by Gab and Nout.

God in the Holy Trinity in Christianity is from eternity, with His Wisdom and His Spirit. There was no time when one of these Person had no existence.

For all the aforementioned reasons, there can be no resemblance between the Holy Trinity of Christianity and the numerous gods of paganism with their variety in sex (a male god and a female goddess) and marriage of gods and begetting children.

(24)

DOES INCARNATION MEAN LIMITATION?

Question:

Does the Incarnation of the Lord mean that He is limited within certain boundaries though He is limitless?

Answer:

Incarnation does not mean limitation, because God is not bounded within a certain place. When He was in the body in a certain place, He was in the Godhead everywhere. It is the same as we say that God was speaking with Moses on the Mountain but He was not only on the Mountain but was at the same time everywhere managing the whole world with its continents. Likewise when God was speaking with Abraham and when He appeared to other prophets, He was at the same time in every other place.

When we say that God is on His throne, we do not mean that He is only on the throne but He is also glorified here and present everywhere. His throne is in heaven, His throne is also in every place where He is glorified. He is in heaven and heaven is not vast enough for Him.

When He spoke to Nicodemus in Jerusalem, He said, "*No one has ascended to heaven but He who came down from heaven, that is, the Son of Man who is in heaven." (John 3:13).* That is, He was in heaven while speaking to Nicodemus in Jerusalem.

He was in the body visible in some place. At the same time in the Godhead He was invisible in other places.

As Godhead He is in every place, but the people see Him in the body in a certain place. This does not contradict with His being in the Godhead in all earth and heaven as the Godhead is unlimited.

(25)

IS CHRIST FOR JEWS ONLY?

Question:

Did the Lord Christ come for the Jews only, the lost sheep of the house of Israel? Can His religion be thus confined to the Jews, not extended to the whole world? And was Judaism also confined to Jews?

Answer:

Religion leads people to God and teaches them about God, about His commandments, the way of worshipping Him and their relationship with Him.

Therefore, any religion should be to the whole world because God is the God of all people and His way is for all people. This is applicable to both Christianity and Judaism.

In Judaism God was not for the Jews alone, but for the whole world. However, the Gentiles did not believe in Him because they were involved in the worship of idols and other gods.

Whoever believed in God, from among the Gentiles, God accepted and did not reject.

A strong evidence of this is the story of Nineveh, a city of Gentiles not Jews to which God sent Jonah the Prophet.

When Nineveh repented and believed through the call of Jonah, God accepted their repentance and faith and said to Jonah, *"And should I not pity Nineveh, that great city?" (Jonah 4:11)*.

Another example is Rahab the Gentile from Jericho and also Ruth the Gentile from Moab. Both of them were accepted by God and were mentioned among the grandmothers of Christ (Matt 1).

The queen of Sheba accepted faith and was married to Solomon the Wise and according to the Ethiopian tradition she begot Menilek from Solomon. There is also the Ethiopian woman whom Moses the Prophet married (Num 12:1). The sailors of the ship which Jonah the prophet rode also accepted faith (Jon 1:16).

There are many other examples in the Old Testament for the conversion of the Gentiles.

As for the New Testament, it is evident that Christianity is for the whole world.

The message of Christ is salvation, for the whole world as the Holy Bible says, *"For God so loved the world that He gave His only begotten Son, that whoever believes in Him should not perish but have everlasting life." (John 3:16)*.

When John the Baptist saw the Lord Christ, he said, "*Behold! The Lamb of God who takes away the sins of the world!*" *(John 1:29)*. The same was repeated by St. John the Evangelist in (1 John 2:2).

To understand the message of the Lord Christ, it is enough to refer to what He said to His holy disciples, "*Go into all the world and preach the gospel to every creature.*" *(Mark 16:15)* and, "*Go therefore and make disciples of all the nations. Baptising them in the name of the Father and of the Son and of the Holy Spirit.*" *(Matt 28:19) and also, "You shall be witnesses to Me in Jerusalem and in all Judea and Samaria and to the end of the earth.*" *(Acts 1:8)*.

The Lord even chose Paul the Apostle to carry His name to the Gentiles, "*I will send you far from here to the Gentiles.*" *(Acts 22:21)*. The Lord said to him also, "*as you have testified for Me in Jerusalem, so you must also bear witness at Rome.*" *(Acts 23:11)*.

About preaching the gospel, the Lord said, "*And this gospel of the kingdom will be preached in all the world as a witness to all the nations.*" *(Matt 24:14)*.

The Lord praised also the faith of the Gentile centurion, saying, "*I have not found such great faith, not even in Israel.*" *(Matt 8:10)* and praised the faith of the Canaanite woman, saying to her, "*great is your faith.*" *(Matt 15:28)*.

The Lord gave as an example of good work the good Samaritan who was better than the priest and the Levite (Luke 10:30-37) and emphasised the fact that the Gentiles are accepted, when He said, *"Many widows were in Israel in the days of Elijah ... but to none of them was Elijah sent except to Zarephath ... to a woman who was a widow." (Luke 4:25, 26)* and likewise with regard to the cleaning of Naaman the Syrian by Elisha the Prophet (Luke 4:27).

The Lord permitted the conversion of Cornelius the Gentile.

The Holy Spirit was poured on Cornelius and those with him so they spoke with tongues (Acts 10:46) and the Lord permitted Philip to baptise the Ethiopian eunuch (Acts 8:27-38).

The father apostles as well in the Council of Jerusalem talked about accepting the Gentiles into faith and explained the way they should be treated (Acts 15). Of course they did not take any decision against God's will.

The whole Book of the Acts of the Apostles tell about the extended preaching to the Gentiles.

The Acts tell us how the apostles spread faith in Asia Minor, in Cyprus, Greece & Italy and reached Spain and other non Jewish countries. Thus, Christianity spread throughout the whole world till it reached us as well as others.

Preaching to the Jews was just a preliminary work, a mere starting point since they have the Law, the symbols and the sayings of the prophets.

But Christianity never said that faith stopped at this starting point not extending farther.

The Lord Christ, preached first amidst the lost sheep of Israel, who had the fathers & the prophets and the Law, but they refused Him. So, it is written, "*but as many as received Him, to them He gave the right to become children of God, to those who believe in His name.*" *(John 1:12)*. The phrase, "as many as received Him" does no refer only to Jews. It was only in the first training missionary that the Lord Christ sent His disciples to the Jews alone, not to the Gentiles or Samaritans, because they were not yet able to bear this at the start of their service.

The Gentiles rejected and despised them and the Samaritans did not deal with them.

The Samaritans once rejected Christ Himself and did not receive Him (Luke 9:53).

Such rejection and enmity on the part of the Samaritans and Gentiles was not fit for the apostles being still beginners in service so as not to find the work hard and fail in performing it.

However, the Lord Christ prepared the way before them to serve Samaria.

He preached to the Samaritan woman and the Samaritan people and they accepted Him. Thus, He said to His disciples, *"I sent you to reap that for which you have not labored." (John 4:38).*

Then He commanded them not to depart from Jerusalem till they have received power from the highest and said to them, *"But you shall receive power when the Holy Spirit has come upon you; and you shall be witnesses to Me in Jerusalem and in all Judea and Samaria and to the end of the earth." (Acts 1:8).*

Notice here the gradual programs that carried their preaching to the end of the earth. However, it is evident that the acceptance of the Gentiles started since the birth of Christ as manifested in the wise men from the East who believed in him and presented their presents to Him and the Lord accepted them.

(26)

WHAT DOES SITTING ON THE RIGHT OF THE FATHER MEAN?

Question:

What is the theological meaning of the words, "He ascended to heaven and sat on the right of the Father?" Does God have right and left as we humans have?

Answer:

By Christ's ascension to heaven is meant His ascension in the body, because the Godhead does not ascend or descend, for He is present in heaven and earth and in between filling all. What the disciples saw was the ascension in the body (Acts 1:9).

As for sitting on the Father's right, God has no right nor left.

The words right and left are said only of limited beings, but God is unlimited. Besides there is no space around Him for anyone to sit in; for He is filling all and present in all places. Furthermore, if the Son sat beside Him, they would be beside each other while the Son said, *"I am in the Father and the Father in Me." (John 14:11)*.

The word "right" in fact, refers to power, greatness and righteousness.

We say in (Ps 118:15-17):
" The right hand of the LORD does valiantly. The right hand of the LORD is exalted; The right hand of the LORD does valiantly. I shall not die, but live."

Likewise, is the case when the righteous will stand on the right of the Lord and the wicked on His left on the Day of Judgement (Matt 25). So, Christ being on the Father's right means in His greatness and righteousness. Therefore, the Lord Christ said to the high priest, *"Hereafter you will see the Son of Man sitting at the right hand of the Power." (Matt 26:64)*.

The word "sitting" here means settled ... settled in the Power.

Hence, the case of making Himself of no reputation (Philem 2:7) ended by the Ascension. Also the spitting, striking and scourging ... etc, ended and He settled in the greatness and when he comes in the second coming He will come in His glory with the holy angels with Him (Matt 25:31), on the clouds of heaven as He ascended (Acts 1:11).

(27)

WHAT IS THE MEANING OF PARTAKERS OF THE DIVINE NATURE?

Question:

What is the meaning of the words "*partakers of the divine nature*" (2 Pet 1:4) and "*the communion of the Holy Spirit*" (2 Cor 13:14)? Do we partake of God's divine nature? Did the human nature unite with the divine nature in the disciples when the Holy Spirit descended on them on the Day of Pentecost?

Answer:

Who partakes of or unites with God in His nature, becomes God! This is against sound faith. Only those who believe in deifying man (in nature not mere title) say this and it is part of the heresy "unity of existence" by which man thinks of himself more highly than he ought to think (Rom 12:3).

The right interpretation of the words "partakers of the divine nature" is the following:

We partake of the divine nature in work, not in essence.

It means that we do not be partakers of the divine nature in the attributes belonging to God alone such as eternity and limitlessness. It is communion in work for the edification of the kingdom whether through our own salvation or winning the others for salvation.

The same may apply to "*the communion of the Holy Spirit*" *(2 Cor 13:14).*

We can never succeed in any work unless God works with us: for, "*Unless the Lord builds the house, they labor in vain who build it.*" *(Ps 127:1).* And in the Travellers Litany we say, "Take part in the work with Your servants."

If God's Spirit takes part in the work with us, we take from Him power and grace and our works be successful and in accordance with God's will, thus we become in "communion with the Holy Spirit" in work.

On the Day of Pentecost, the gifts of the Holy Spirit poured on the disciples.

This realised the prophecy of Joel the prophet, "*I will pour out of My Spirit on all flesh: your sons and your daughters shall prophesy, your young men shall see visions, your old men shall dream dreams.*" *(Acts 2:17, Joe 2:28).* It was also a realisation of the Lord's promise to His disciples, "*But you shall receive power when the Holy Spirit has come upon you and you shall be witnesses to Me." (Acts 1:8).* Speaking in tongues was among the gifts God granted them (Acts 2:6). This gift of speaking languages helped spread faith.

The unity of the divine nature and the human nature happened only in the Incarnation of the Lord Christ alone.

Can it be believed, then, that all the disciples became like Christ on the Day of Pentecost?

Here we face a question: What distinguishes Christ from others?

The divinity of Christ is attacked in two ways:

a) Either lowering Christ to the level of ordinary humans as the Arians did; or

b) Raising humans to the level of Christ as those who believe in the philosophy of deification of man proclaim on the ground that the nature of humans united with the nature of God!

If we say that man united with the divine nature, it means that he became God and became infallible. In this case he does not sin, he is not mere human.

But the action of God's Spirit in man is one thing and the unity between God's nature and man's nature is something different. We do not unite with God's nature. Let's be humble and behave as humans as our father Abraham said about himself that he is dust and ashes (Gen 18:7) and as Job the Righteous also said (Job 42:6).

(28)

HAVE CHRIST'S MIRACLES BEEN WORKED BY IMPRESSION?

Question:

What is your opinion of saying that Christ's miracles have been worked by impression?

Answer:

Impression is an influence on one's heart and thoughts to be convinced of something,
but:

1. Can there be any relation between impression and raising of the dead?

A person may impress a living person and influence his heart and thoughts, but cannot have any influence on the dead whereas the Lord Christ raised the dead such as the daughter of Jairus (Mark 5:41, 42), the son of the Widow of Nain (Luke 7:11-17) and Lazarus (John 11:17-44) and all of these are of course beyond impression.

The son of Nain was raised by Christ while carried in a bier on the way and Lazarus was raised after four days in the tomb in front of the consolers. Did the impression extend to the consolers and to those who escorted the dead? Or did the impression enter into the tomb or the bier of the dead to influence him?

2. No relation is there between impression and the insane or possessed.

How can one impress an insane who has no control over his mind and feelings? or impress a possessed who is controlled by the devils?

The Lord Christ healed many insane such as the demon - possessed, blind and mute (Matt 12:22) and the insane of the country of the Gadarenes who was seized by the demons and was always bound with chains and shackles and was driven by many demons (Legion) (Luke 8:29-32), can such a person be influenced by an outer impression?

3. No relation is there between impression and casting out of unclean spirits.

An unclean spirit cannot be impressed, we have an amazing example the man with the unclean spirit who was crying out but the Lord Christ rebuked him, saying, " Be quiet, and come out of him!" And when the unclean spirit had convulsed him and cried out with a loud voice, he came out of him. Then they were all amazed, so that they questioned among themselves, saying, *"What is this? What new doctrine is this? For with authority He commands even the unclean spirits, and they obey Him." (Mark 1:25-27)*.

What impression is here? This miracle was in the Synagogue in Capernaum in front of all the people there and they felt the power and authority of Christ. The same happened when the Lord healed the mute demon-possessed man. He cast out the demon and the man spoke, so the multitude marvelled, saying, *"It was never seen like this in Israel." (Matt 9:32,33)*.

In another miracle of healing, the Lord Christ rebuked the unclean spirit, saying, *"You deaf and dumb spirit, I command you, come out of him and enter him no more." (Mark 9:25, 27)* and the man was cured from that very hour (Matt 17:18).

4. No relation also is there between impression and nature: sea, wind and trees.

Even if it is possible to have impression on rational beings, it is completely impossible to have impression on non living and non rational beings.

For example the fig tree, which represents hypocrisy, which the Lord Christ cursed, saying, *"Let no one eat fruit from you ever again." (Mark 11:14)* and immediately the tree withered away (Matt 21:19). Did it wither by impression? And when the great tempest arose on the sea and the boat was covered with the waves, the Lord Christ *"arose and rebuked the wind and said to the sea, 'Peace, be still!' and the- wind ceased and there was a great calm." (Mark 4:39).* Is it by impression or through authority over nature? Let the greatest psychologists in the world calm a stormy sea through impression.

Besides the nature miracles, there are the miracles of fishing.

The first miracle was with Peter the Apostle before being invited. He had spent the whole night without catching any fish, but on the word of Christ the fish increased and filled the two boats till they began to sink because of the great number of fish (Luke 5:1-7).

The second miracle was after the Resurrection (John 21:10-14). Of course the fish did not come suddenly into the net due to an impression but upon the word of Christ!!

5. No impression is there in healing a person from afar.

The Lord Christ healed the daughter of the Canaanite woman at the request of her mother. That daughter in her home had not been under any impression. The Lord-glory be to Him- said to the Canaanite woman, "Go your way, the demon has gone out of your daughter." And when she had come to her house, she found the demon gone out and her daughter lying on the bed (Mark 7:29-30). In the same way the Lord said to the king's nobleman, *"Go your way, your son lives." (John 4:50)* and the son was healed from that hour though he was at home not exposed to an impression. Likewise the centurion's servant was healed through the word of Christ from far away (Matt 8:13).

6. Creating works as well cannot be performed by impression.

Feeding the four thousand men besides women and children by seven loaves and a few little fish (Matt 15:32-38) cannot be by impression. Moreover, seven large baskets were left full of the fragments which means that a new substance was created.
And the feeding of the five thousand men, besides women and children by five loaves and two fish cannot have been by impression! Even if they had the impression that they were filled, how would there remain twelve baskets full (Matt 14:20)? From where had such a quantity come unless they were created by a miracle not by impression?

The same happened in the miracle of giving sight to the man born blind.

The Lord Christ created eyes to him, a matter which cannot have been performed by impression especially that the way Christ used for this was capable to cause the opposite! The Lord put clay on the eyes of the blind man and this may cause blindness to one having sight! Then He ordered him to go and wash in the pool of Siloam (John 9:6, 7). Such washing was easy to remove clay not to create an eye with tissues and nerves!! The clay cannot be a means of giving impression of sight to the man!

In the same way the water was turned into wine by a miracle.

The Lord created a substance that was not before, because water has not the compounds of wine. He did this without any process whatsoever; He just said, *"Fill the water pots with water." (John 2:7) then said, "Draw some out now...."* Thus, a new substance was created by the Lord's mere will. There was no impression because the guests who drank it knew nothing about what had happened, it was done by the servants not by one of the guests. Where is the impression then?

7. Healing of infirmities cannot be effected by impression.

A blind cannot have sight by impression or a lame have a leg by impression: nor a dumb, a mute or a deaf can be healed by impression.

The Lord Christ worked many such miracles. For the blind, He healed Bartimaeus (Mark 10:52) and another one with him (Matt 20:34). He healed the blind man of Bethsaida (Mark 8:22-26), the blind and mute man (Matt 12:22) and two blind men (Matt 9:27-31).

He healed the deaf and the mute (Mark 7:31, 37), (Matt 9:32-33), (Luke 19:42) and many other examples such as healing the ear of Malchus the servant of the high priest which was cut off by someone (Luke 22:50, 51).

8. Healing of the leper cannot be effected by impression.

The leper had to stay away from the community and when he is healed the priest examines him to make sure that he got well so he can be allowed to join the community after offering a sacrifice. However, the Lord Christ healed the leper by a touch of his hand and immediately they were cleansed (Mark 1:41) (Matt 8:2,3). He healed ten leper men at one time (Luke 17:11-19) and they showed themselves to the priests as usual. Were the priests also under impression?

Many other incurable diseases were healed by Christ.

9. No impression can be effected in case of so many miracles and so many onlookers.

Perhaps one person may come under impression and be influenced, but when hundreds of people with various diseases and different psychological and mental abilities are healed, the matter becomes different as in the miracles worked by Christ.
St. Luke the Evangelist says, *"When the sun was setting, all those who had any that were sick with various diseases brought them to Him; and He laid His hands on every one of them and healed them." (Luke 4:40, 41).*

St. Matthew the Evangelist says about the Lord that He was *"healing all kinds of sickness and all kinds of disease among the people." (Matt 4:23).* And St. Mark the Evangelist says, *"they brought to Him all who were sick and those who were demon-possessed. And the whole city was gathered together at the door. Then He healed many who were sick with various diseases and cast out many demons." (Mark 1:32-34).*

Were all those and the onlookers as well "under impression"?

10. The miracles that happened in the life of Christ Himself could not have been due to impression.

Such miracles as His Resurrection, His appearance to eleven then to all His disciples, His transfiguration, His virgin birth... etc., all such miracles could not have been due to impression.

(29)

DID CHRIST WORK HIS MIRACLES BY PRAYER?

Question:

Did Christ pray before working the miracle so that God might do it and respond to His prayer?

Answer:

If we examine the miracles worked by Christ, we shall find the opposite.

He healed diseases just by a command from Him not by prayer.

✣ To the paralytic He said, "*Arise, take up your bed and go to your house.*" *(Matt 9:6-8)* and he arose and departed to his house.

✣ To the man at Bethesda who had an infirmity thirty-eight years, He said the same words, "*Rise, take up your bed and walk*" *and immediately the man was made well, took up his bed and walked (John 5:8, 9).*

✣ To the man with the withered hand He said, "*Stretch out your hand, and he stretched it out and it was restored as whole as the other." (Mark 3:5).*

✣ When Simon's wife's mother was sick with a high fever, He rebuked the fever and it left her immediately and she arose and served them (Luke 4:38) (Mark 1:31).

By command also He had power over unclean spirits and over nature.

He ordered the unclean spirits to come out as in (Mark 9:25, 27), when He said, "*You deaf and dumb spirit, I command you, come out of him.*" And when He rebuked the unclean spirit and the spirit came out the people were amazed and said, "*with authority He commands even the unclean spirits and they obey Him." (Mark 1:27).* What prayer did he say at that time? He even rebuked He wind and the waves and there was a great calm by His command (Mark 4:39).

He raised the dead by His command.

He raised the son of the widow of Nain while in the coffin, saying to him, "*Young man, I say to you, arise*" *and the dead young man sat up and began to speak (Luke 7:14, 15).* In the same way He raised the daughter of Jairus, one of the rulers of the Synagogue, commanding her, "*Little girl, I say to you, arise*", and immediately the girl arose and walked *(Mark 5:41, Lu 8:54, 55).* No mention was made of prayer in both cases.

He healed some of the sick by laying His hands on them.

"He laid His hands on every one of them and healed them." (Luke 4:40). When healing the deaf man, He put His fingers in the man's ears and said, "Ephphatha i.e. be opened" and immediately his ears were opened and he was healed (Mark 7:35). He put His hands on the blind man of Betheseda and the man restored his sight (Mark 8:25).

And He laid His hands on the woman who had a spirit of infirmity for eighteen years that made her bent over and she was healed immediately (Luke 13:13). He just touched the ear of Malchus the servant of the high priest and it was healed (Luke 22:51). He touched the eyes of the two blind man and immediately their eyes received sight and they followed him (Matt 20:34). In all these miracles it is not mentioned that He prayed.

By a mere touch from Him, the sick was healed without any prayer.

The woman who had a flow of blood for twelve years and spent all that she had and was no better, when she just touched His garment, *"Immediately the fountain of her blood was dried up .... she was healed." (Mark 5:29).*

St. Mark the Evangelist put it so wonderfully, saying, "Wherever he entered, into villages, cities, or the country, they *laid the sick in the market places and begged Him that they might just touch the border of His garment. And as many as touched Him were made well." (Mark 6:56).*

A mere touch, a mere word, without any prayer from the Lord Christ nor from the sick person healed the sick.

When the leper implored Him, saying, "If You are willing, You can make me clean." The Lord was moved with compassion, put out His hand and touched him, saying, *"I am willing, be cleaned" and immediately the leprosy left him and he was cleaned (Mark 1:41) (Matt 8:2, 3).* There was no prayer at all but His mere willing.

By His mere willing water turned into wine and a new substance was created

He said to the servants, "Fill the water pots with water." Then He said, *"Draw some out now" and it was good wine (John 2:7, 8).* This happened because He just willed it, without any prayer.

Furthermore, is there any prayer in the miracles of His reading the thoughts of others and telling about unknown things.

When healing the paralytic, He read the thoughts of the scribes who were reasoning within their hearts against Him and replied to them (Mark 2:6-11). When the sinful woman washed His feet with her tears and wiped them with her hair, Simon the

Pharisee spoke in his heart against the Lord, but the Lord knew Simon's thoughts and answered him (Luke 7:39-47). Many times also He answered to the thoughts of His disciples.

Without prayer also he knew the unknown as when He told Peter about the piece of money in the fish which would come first in his hook (Matt 17:24-27) and as He knew that Nathanael had been put under the fig tree (John 1:48, 49).

The only miracle for which He prayed was the raising of Lazarus from the dead (John 11:41, 42).

Perhaps the cause was to conceal His divinity from the devil because there were only a few days before crucifixion. And perhaps one miracle by prayer from among so many miracles without prayers was meant to teach us to pray. It may be also an answer to His enemies who accused Him of doing His miracles by the power of the devils. However, even in the miracle of raising Lazarus, He commanded him, crying with a loud voice, "*Lazarus, come forth!*" *(John 11:43).*

In the miracle of feeding the multitude, it is stated that He looked up to heaven, blessed and broke the loaves (Mark 6:41; Mt 15:36).

It was not mentioned in both miracles that He prayed. As for looking up and blessing food before eating, it may be to teach us to do the same.

(30)

IS THE TITLE "SON OF MAN" AGAINST CHRIST'S DIVINITY?

Question:

Why did the Lord Christ call Himself the Son of Man? Is it a denial of His divinity? Why did He not say that He is the Son of God?

Answer:

The Lord Christ called Himself the Son of God and He called Himself also the Son of Man.

He called Himself the Son of God in His talk with the man born blind, so the man believed in Him and worshipped Him (John 9:35-38). Sometimes, He called Himself the Son in such a way that proves His divinity as when He said, *".. that all should honour the Son just as they honour the Father" (John 5:21-23) and, " no one knows who the Son is except the Father, and who the Father is except the Son, and the one to whom the Son wills to reveal Him." (Luke 10:22) and He said about Himself, "If the Son makes you free, you shall be free indeed." (John 8:36).*

The Lord Christ accepted to be called the Son of God and made this the basis of faith blessing Peter for this confession.

He accepted this title from Nathanael (John 1:49) and from those who saw Him walking on the water (Matt 14:33). He blessed St. Peter when he said, *"You are the Christ, the Son of the living God." Jesus answered and said to him, "Blessed are you, Simon Bar-Jonah, for flesh and blood has not revealed this to you, but My Father who is in heaven." (Matt 16:16, 17).*

There are many testimonies in the Holy Bible that Christ is the Son of God.

The gospel of St. Mark starts with the words, *"The beginning of the gospel of Jesus Christ, the Son of God." (Mark 1:1).* And the angel, when announcing the Virgin of the holy birth, said to her, *"therefore, also, that Holy One who is to be born will be called the Son of God." (Luke 1:35).* The Father Himself testified for Him at the time of His baptism (Matt 3:17) and on the Mount of Transfiguration (Mark 9:7); (2 Pe 1:17, 18).

In the story of the wicked tenants, the Father said, *"I will send My beloved Son." (Luke 20:13)* and said in the prophecy, *"Out of Egypt I have called My Son." (Matt 2:15).* St. Paul the Apostle preached the same (Acts 9:20) and St. John the Apostle (1 Jo 4:15) and the other apostles as well.

So, He was not only called the Son of Man, but also the Son of God, the Son and the Only Begotten Son.

This is explained in detail in the answer to the question about the difference between our being God's children and Christ being the Son of God.

The Lord Christ used the name Son of Man on occasions demonstrating His divinity.

1. As Son of Man He has the power to forgive sins.

This is clear in His talk with the scribes in the miracle of healing the paralytic. He said to them, *"But that you may know that the Son of Man has power on earth to forgive sins"; then He said to the paralytic, "Arise, take up your bed, and go to your house." (Matt 9:2-6)*.

2. As Son of Man He is present in heaven and on earth at the same time.

He said to Nicodemus, *"No one has ascended to heaven but He who came down from heaven, that is, the Son of Man who is in heaven." (John 3:13)*. Thus He showed that He is in heaven while talking to Nicodemus on earth, which proves His divinity.

3. He said that the Son of Man is the Lord of the Sabbath.

When the Pharisees blamed Him because His disciples plucked heads of grain on the Sabbath when they were hungry, saying to Him, "Look, your disciples are doing what is not lawful to do on the Sabbath" He explained the matter, saying, *"For the Son of Man is Lord even of the Sabbath." (Matt 12:8)*. And of course God is the Lord of the Sabbath.

4. He said that the angels were ascending and descending on the Son of Man.

When Nathanael was amazed because the Lord knew the unknown i.e. His being under the fig tree and said to Him, *"Rabbi, You are the Son of God." The Lord did not deny that He is the Son of God, but said to him, "You will see greater things than these ... you shall see heaven open, and the angels of God ascending and descending upon the Son of Man." (John 1:48-51)*. So, the term "Son of Man" here does not mean an ordinary man but a person having the divine dignity.

5. He said that the Son of Man will sit on the right hand of Power and will come on the clouds of heaven.

When He was being tried and the high priest said to Him, *"I put You under oath by the living God: Tell us if You are the Christ, the Son of God!" Jesus said to him, "It is as you said. Nevertheless, I say to you, hereafter you will see the Son of Man sitting at the right hand of the Power, and coming on the clouds of heaven." (Matt 26:63-65)*. The high priest tore his clothes, saying, "He has spoken blasphemy! What further need do we have of witnesses? Look, now you have heard His blasphemy!

The same testimony was made by St. Stephen; for at the time of his being martyred, he said, "*Look, I see the heavens opened and the Son of Man standing at the right hand of God.*" *(Acts 7:56)* .

6. He said that He - Son of Man - will judge the world.

Though it is well known that God is, "*the Judge of all the world.*" *(Gen 18:25),* the Lord Christ said about His second coming, "*For the Son of Man will come in the glory of His Father with His angels and then He will reward each according to His works.*" *(Matt 16:27).* Notice also that He said about the angels "His angels" whereas they are God's angels.

There is also an implied theological meaning in the words "the glory of His Father" i.e.:

7. He said that He is the Son of God having the glory of His Father at the same time of being the Son of Man.

The Son of Man will come in the glory of God His Father i.e. He is Son of Man and Son of God at the same time having the same glory of His Father. How wonderful it is to say these words about Him as Son of Man. So, this title does not prejudice His divinity.

8. As Son of Man He will judge the world and will be addressed as "Lord".

He said, "When the Son of Man comes in His glory and all the holy angels with Him, then He will sit on the throne of His glory. All the nations will be gathered before Him... He will set the sheep on His right hand, but the goats on the left. Then the King will say to those on His right hand, *"Come, you blessed of My Father, inherit the Kingdom prepared for you... saying, 'Lord, when ...' Then the righteous will answer Him, saying, 'when did we see You hungry and feed You...'"* (Matt 25:31-37). The word "Lord" prove His divinity and the words "My Father" prove that being Son of Man He is also Son of God.

He says also, *"Watch therefore, for you do not know what hour your Lord is coming"* (Matt 24:42). Who is that Lord? In (Matt 25:13) He says, *"Watch therefore, for you know neither the day nor the hour in which the Son of Man is coming."* So, He used the words "your Lord" and "Son of Man" in the same meaning.

9. As Son of Man He calls the angels His angels and the elect His elect and the kingdom His kingdom.

He says about the signs of the end of ages, *"Immediately after the tribulation of those days... Then the sign of the Son of Man will appear in heaven ... and they will see the Son of Man coming on the clouds of heaven with power and great glory.*

And He will send His angels with a great sound of a trumpet and they will gather together His lect..." (Matt 24:29-31). And He says about the end of the ages, *"the Son of Man will send out His angels and they will gather out of His kingdom all things that offend and those who practice lawlessness and will cast them into the furnace of fire." (Matt 13:40, 41).* Of course it is evident that the angels are God's angels (John 1:51) and the kingdom is God's kingdom (Mark 9:1) and the elect are God's elect.

10. He speaks about believing in Him as Son of Man with the same words He spoke about believing in Him as the Only Begotten Son of God.

He says, *"And as Moses lifted up the serpent in the wilderness, even so must the Son of Man be lifted up, that whoever believes in Him should not perish but have eternal life. For God so loved the world that He gave His only begotten Son, that whoever believes in Him should not perish but have everlasting life." (John 3:14-16).*

Is it necessary that people believe in an ordinary son of Man so as to have everlasting life? It is evident here that what is said about the Son of Man is the same concerning the only begotten Son of God.

11. Daniel's prophecy about Him as Son of Man refers to His divinity.

Daniel said, "I was watching in the night visions and behold, One like the Son of Man, coming with the clouds of heaven! He came to the Ancient of Days and they brought Him before Him. Then to Him was given dominion and glory and a kingdom, that all peoples, nations and languages should serve Him. His dominion is an everlasting dominion, which shall not pass away and His kingdom the one which shall not be destroyed." (Dan 7:13, 14). Who but God is served by all peoples, nations and languages and have everlasting dominion and kingdom?

12. He said about Himself in the Revelation that He is the Alpha and the Omega, the First and the Last.

St. John the Visionary said and in the midst of the seven lamp stands, *"One like the Son of Man,... He laid His right hand on me, saying to me, 'Do not be afraid; I am the First and the Last. I am He who lives and was dead and behold, I am alive forevermore. Amen.'" (Rev 1:13-18).* And at the end of the Revelation He said, *"And behold, I am coming quickly and My reward is with Me, to give every one according to his work. I am the Alpha and the Omega, the Beginning and the End, the First and the Last." (Rev 22:12, 13).*

All these are titles of God Himself (Is 48:12, 44:6).

Since all these verses prove His divinity, why then did He call Himself the Son of Man concentrating on this title?

He called Himself Son of Man because He was to carry out redemption on behalf of man.

He came for this purpose, to save the world through bearing the sins of all humanity.

He explained this when He said, *"For the Son of Man has come to save that which was lost." (Matt 18:11).*

The death sentence was issued against man, so, who should die was man. Hence Christ came to die, being Son of Man, i.e. the Son of that man in particular who was sentenced to death. Therefore He called Himself Son of Man. He is the Son of Man and in this attribute He should suffer, be crucified and die to redeem us.

That is why He said, *"The Son of Man is about to be betrayed into the hands of man and they will kill him and the third day He will be raised up." (Matt 17:22,23;26:45)* and, *"the Son of Man must suffer many things and be rejected by the elders and Chief priests and scribes and be killed and after three days rise again." (Mark 8:31).*

Indeed, His message as Son of Man was this: ***"The Son of Man has come to save that which was lost." (Matt 18:11).***

(31)

SPIRITUALISM

Question:

What is your opinion concerning spiritualism? What is the rule of religion with respect to it? Can anyone call spirits, ask them and receive their answers and believe what they say?

Answer:

The first point is: How far can a person call a spirit?
This question entails two other questions:

1. Do humans have authority to move spirits as they wish from their place?

2. Do spirits have freedom to move at any call?

We know that the spirits of the righteous go to Paradise as the Lord said to the thief on His right hand, *"Today, you will be with Me in Paradise." (Luke 23:43)*. Do we then have such a power as to bring a righteous spirit from Paradise though these spirits are in a higher and better state than ours? How can we move the spirits of the saints and stop their contemplations just to satisfy our curiosity asking them questions perhaps on trivialities and occupying them with worldly matters after having departed from our World?

We inquire also: Do these spirits move by God's permission?

It is impossible that the spirits of the righteous move from Paradise without God's permission. God may send the spirits of some saints to render some service to the people on earth as He sends the angels for the same purpose (Heb 1:14). But for us to call these spirits to see them it is another thing we have no authority to do, especially that God hates calling up the dead and considers this abominations as well as magic and conjuring (Deut 18:9-12).

The spirits of the righteous are commanded in God's hands.

The Lord Christ said this about His human spirit (Luke 23:46) and St. Stephan said it while being martyred, *"Lord Jesus, receive my spirit." (Acts 7:59).*

How then can any person call these spirits in his own way though he might be unbeliever? What authority can a person have in this regard?

Do this calling of the spirits conform withthe rest which the righteous have in Paradise?

Our father Abraham did not permit Lazarus to return to the world not even to do good.

When the rich man asked father Abraham to send Lazarus to advise his brothers to avoid the same end, our father Abraham refused, saying, *"They have Moses and the prophets." (Luke 16:29).* Can then spirits come to us at the call of humans without permission from God who hates this just to answer the questions of the people and satisfy their curiosity? Can this be something usual practised by many who claim that they called hundreds and thousands of spirits and recorded their confessions?

As regards the evil spirits, they are imprisoned - as we know - in Hades without any rest.

So, we inquire: How can these sinful spirits come out of their prison i.e. Hades.

How can they come out of Hades to meet their friends, acquaintances or relatives and speak with them as if on a picnic or enjoying their time? They do not deserve this nor
can do it, they or those calling them, because it is not within their power and they are thinking more highly than they ought to think (Rom 12:30).

A human spirit cannot move freely as it wishes.

It is stated in the Scriptures about death, *"Then the dust will return to the earth as it was and the spirit will return to God who gave it." (Eccl 12:7).* So, since the spirit returns to God, it may not have any power to disobey Him or not return to Him! *"No one has power over the spirit to retain the spirit." (Eccl 8:8)* and also, *"You take away their breath, they die and return to their dust." (Ps 104:29).* And since their breath is taken away from them, then they have no power over themselves. St. Peter the Apostle says about the spirits in Hades, *"the spirits in the prison." (1 Pet 3:19),* who then have power to bring a spirit out of prison to talk with it?

Furthermore, there is no text in the Holy Bible showing that spirits move freely as they wish not as God wills.

The Bible says that Lazarus died and the angels carried him to Abraham's bosom (Luke 16:22), whereas the rich man died, was buried and talked from Hades (Luke 16:23). If he was able to have contact with his relatives, he would not pray Abraham to send Lazarus to them.

How can the spiritists be sure that they are human spirits?

Truly said that these spirits need to identify themselves. How can you make sure that they are human spirits? Is it because they tell information and secrets? The devil also knows the past and can imitate voices and forms. And if the devil can transform himself into an angel of light, can he not assume the form of man?

What about the methods used by the spiritist?

Do the methods reveal the human power or God's power? Can we describe such methods as spiritual work though they are against God's commandment (Deut 18:9-12).

This may be a brief answer to the question, but I may return to other points on the same topic while answering other questions.

(32)

MAY THE DEVIL BE SAVED?

Question:

I heard from some people that the devil may be saved! They claimed that some fathers said this. Is this thought right?

Answer:

The devil cannot be saved. There are even explicit texts in the Holy Bible supporting our view. One of the most important of these is in the Revelation, *"And the devil, who deceived them, was cast into the lake of fire and brimstone where the beast and the false prophet are. And they will be tormented day and night forever and ever." (Rev 20:10).*

The text is clear that the devil will perish forever in the lake of fire and brimstone. So, any proclamation that the devil will be saved is a heresy against the biblical doctrine to which should apply the words of St. Paul the Apostle, *"But even if we, or an angel from heaven, preach any other gospel to you than what we have preached to you, let him be accursed" (Gal 1:8,9).*

As regards the sayings of the fathers in this respect, it is impossible that a father of sound faith proclaims teaching against the Bible.

However, one of the accusations against the scholar Origen was that he proclaimed the salvation of the devil. But Origen's friends tried to defend him concerning this point by providing quotations from his works against this heresy.

For more elucidation we say that the devil is resistant to God and His kingdom.

Since the beginning, now and in future he is resistant.

Since his fall he led astray a group of angels and made them fall. Then he led astray our forefathers and the whole humanity until: *"There is none who does good, No, not one." (Ps 14:3).*

Suffice that he dared to ask the Lord Christ Himself to fall down and worship him (Matt 4:9). His resistance made an angel cry out, saying, *"The Lord rebuke you. Satan! The Lord ... rebuke you." (Zech 3:2; Jg 9).*

Even after being bound one thousand years, the devil did not learn the lesson nor changed his conduct, but continued in his wickedness.

St. John the Beloved says in the Revelation, *"Then I saw an angel coming down from heaven ... and a great chain in his hand. He laid hold of the dragon, that serpent of old, who is the Devil and Satan and bound him for a thousand years; and he cast him into the bottomless pit." (Rev 20:1-3).*

However, after being released from his prison, he went out to deceive the nations (Rev 20:7, 8).

The devil will try, very violently, on the last days, to do away with God's Kingdom, but God will interfere.

The Lord Christ, speaking about the end of ages, says *"and unless those days were shortened, no flesh would be saved, but for the elect's sake those days will be shortened." (Matt 24:22), For false christs and false prophets will arise and show great signs and wonders, so as to deceive, if possible, even the elect." (Matt 24:24).*

The wonders that are worked by those who are led astray are in fact worked by the devil.

St. Paul the Apostle - speaking about the man of sin, the son of perdition, who opposes and exalts himself above all that is called God and who will be the cause of the last great apostasy - says, *"The coming of the lawless one is according to the working of Satan, with all power, signs and lying wonders and with all unrighteous deception among those who perish." (2 Thess 2:9).*

God will send the archangel Michael to fight the devil and his evil angels and overcome them.

St. John the Visionary says and war broke out in heaven: Michael and his angels fought against the dragon: and the dragon and his angels fought, but they did not prevail, nor was a place found for them in heaven any longer. So the great dragon was cast out, that serpent of old, called the Devil and Satan, who deceives the whole world, he was cast to the earth and his angels were cast out with him. Then I heard a loud voice saying in heaven, *"Now salvation and strength and the kingdom of our God and the power of His Christ have come, for the accuser of our brethren, who accused them before our God day and night, has been cast down." (Rev 12:7-10).*

This is the famous icon that shows the archangel Michael with the sword of justice in his hand trodding on the devil.

Yet, even after such a defeat, the devil continued fighting (Rev 12:13) till God cast him into the lake of fire and brimstone where he was tormented with his assistants forever and ever (Rev 20: 10).

The perdition of the devil and the impossibility of his salvation is proved by the words of the Lord Christ to those on His left hand on the Day of Judgement: *"Depart from Me, you cursed, into the everlasting fire prepared for the devil and his angels." (Matt 25:41).*

If God has prepared such everlasting fire for the devil and his angels, how then would he be saved? In all the preceding texts we notice the perdition of the devil, his torment and the everlasting perdition.

Certainly the devils know their end.

That is why St. James the Apostle says that they tremble (Jas 2:19). And the demons cast out by the Lord in the country of Gergesenes cried out, *"What have we to do with You, Jesus, You Son of God? Have You come here to torment us before the time?" (Matt 8:29).*

No religion has a different view concerning the torment of the devils.

It is a matter of course supported by the texts of the Holy Bible. And if it is possible - supposing the impossible - that the devil be saved, there would have been in the Holy Bible even one sentence or reference to such an amazing event.

Moreover, if the devil is saved, none else would perish.

It is because no one has ever done more evil than the devil. But non perdition of everyone is against the teachings of the Bible.

(33)

THOSE WHOM THE CHURCH DOES NOT PRAY FOR.

Question:

Who are those whom the Church does not pray for after their death? Why? And can the church pray for the person who commits suicide, being with mental and psychological disorder?

Answer:

The church may not pray for a person who died in sin without having repented and if they prayed for him wrongly he will not benefit from the prayer.

We know that the wages of sin is death as the Holy Bible says (Rom 6:23). So, if the sinner does not repent for his sin he will be subject to the words of the Lord Christ, *"Unless you repent you will all likewise perish." (Luke 13:3)*.

The words of St. John the Apostle support the view that no prayer should be raised for one who dies in sin, St. John says, *"There is sin leading to death. I do not say that he should pray about that." (1 John 5:16)*.

Examples of those who die in sin and the Church does not pray for them:

+ Suppose a thief climbed up a water pipe of some house to steal but he fell dead; the church does not pray for such a person because he died while sinning.

+ A smuggler of drugs is seized by the policemen and they shot at one another, the smuggler and others died in the fight: the church does not pray for him.

+ A person died while being drunken, or a dancer died in an uninnocent pastime evening, or a person died while quarrelling with others in gambling: Those and the alike are not prayed for by the church.

+ A person who dies in apostasy or while proclaiming a heresy or hesitancy without repenting.

+ Who commits suicide is not prayed for by the Church.

Why does the church not pray for the person who commits suicide?

Who commits suicide is a murderer and he does not own his life to put an end to it. By murdering himself he had committed a crime and did not repent for it.

Who commits suicide has lost faith in the other life thinking that death will end his troubles. He does not believe that death opens before him another life in which he is received as murderer and will go to Hades and will suffer torments harder than his troubles on earth. If he has such a belief he would fear death instead of seeking it as a solution.

Who commits suicide has lost hope which is one of three greatest virtues ie. Faith, Hope & Love (1 Cor 13:13). Losing hope is another sin added to murdering and Judas fell in it.

Who commits suicide has lost forbearance and patience till the end.

Who commits suicide has died lacking the virtues of consulting others and obedience, because any believer who is honest in his confession, obedient to his father confessor cannot perish. True indeed are the words of the Wiseman.

If the church prays for a person who commits suicide, it will be considered as if encouraging suicide.

The only exception for not praying for the person committing suicide is the case in which his madness is established.

If the person who commits suicide has complete mental disorder, he will not be responsible for his behaviour. Likewise, if he has no will nor freedom, because responsibility requires that one be wise, free and willing.

The church may not console the family of the person who committed suicide.

If the church consoles his family, it will be a kind of hypocrisy. We may only say that we hope if that person was at the time of his committing suicide was insane and irresponsible and ask God to have compassion for his state of mind. But no absolution nor prayer of the departed should be prayed for him.

We leave the matter concerning the person who committed suicide in God's hands who is the Most Merciful.

We should trust that when God judges anyone, He takes into consideration all his circumstances; whether the mental, psychological or nervous. God judges according to His limitless wisdom and knowledge. This is beyond our responsibility as Church.

Not only committing suicide has psychological factors but all other sins as well.

Every sin has psychological factors leading to it, but God knows everything. Every sin, like that of committing suicide, proves that its doer is not soundly thinking. Therefore, we pray God for fooleries of His people and the Holy Bible calls the sinner fool, even the atheist who may be a philosopher. It is written about all those, *"The fool has said in his heart: There is no God." (Ps 14:1)*.

We may ask forgiveness for any sin that might have been repented for.

For example, we may pray for the person who commits suicide but does not die immediately, such as a person who stabs himself but dies after one day or some hours. Such a person may have repented for this sin before his death. Someone else may burn himself for example, but is saved and dies a few days afterwards affected by his burns that could not be healed by medicine; such a person may also be prayed for. Similar cases may be prayed for likewise.

(34)

THOSE WHO WERE FORGIVEN BEFORE THE CROSS

Question:

The Lord Christ said to the paralytic, "*your sins are forgiven you.*" *(Mark 2:5) and to the sinful woman He said the same (Luke 7:48).* Both obtained forgiveness without baptism nor confession, in the same moment, what is the necessity of these two sacraments then?

Answer:

The Holy Bible says, "*Without shedding of blood there is no remission.*" *(Heb 9:22).* So, the sins of the paralytic and the sinful woman were only forgiven on the cross, not in the same moment and likewise every forgiveness granted before the crucifixion. **It is only a promise of forgiveness, not attainment of forgiveness.**

The same can be said with regard to those who offered sacrifices in the Old Testament with repentance for forgiveness of their sins. They waited in Hades with all the righteous of the Old Testament until Christ was crucified and saved them. It is written about them, *"not having received the promises, but having seen them afar off were assured of them, embraced them." (Heb 11:13)*.

Thus, the paralytic and the sinful woman did not obtain forgiveness before the crucifixion, but they deserved it and took a document of the promise.

There is one question: **Have they died before or after the crucifixion?**

If they have died before the crucifixion, they had to wait in Hades till Christ was crucified. And whoever died before the crucifixion was not required to be baptised the New Testament baptism which is based on the deserts of the blood of Christ; for baptism is also death and resurrection with Christ as the apostle said, *".... we were buried with Him through baptism into death." (Rom 6:4)*. Before the crucifixion Christ had not been buried nor His blood shed and therefore no need for baptism.

But if those two (ie. the paralytic and the sinful woman) had lived till the foundation of the church, they would have been required to believe in Christ's redemption, crucifixion and resurrection and to be baptised since they came to know this sacrament. They would be subject to the words of the Lord, *"He who believes and is baptised will be saved." (Mark 16:16)* and to the words of St. Peter the Apostle, *"Repent and let every one of you be baptised in the name of Jesus Christ for the remission of sins." (Acts 2:38).* They had also to walk in a sound spiritual life and the words, "your sins are forgiven you" would be for their old sins only and every new sin would require repentance, confession and holy communion according to the Holy Bible.

(35)

HOW CAN IT BE THAT CHRIST PRAYS & GETS TIRED?

Question:

Is it against the Lord Christ's divinity that He prayed and got tired sometimes? How can we interpret His praying, His fatigue and similar things?

Answer:

Those addressing these questions concentrate on Christ's divinity and forget His humanity!

He is not only God, but He also took on Him a human nature like ours; a complete human nature. Hence it is written that He shared with us everything except sin (Heb 2:17) and unless He had taken our nature, He would not have been able to satisfy the divine justice on our behalf.

He prayed as Man not as God.

He presented to us the ideal Man. If He had not prayed He would not have been an example, so He prayed.

With His prayer He taught us to pray and how to pray.

He gave us a practical idea about the importance and the value of prayers in our life. In some of His prayers, as in Gethsemane, He even taught us how to struggle in prayers Luke 22:44).

If Christ had not prayed, this would have been an accusation against Him.

The scribes and Pharisees would have considered Him far from spirituality and would have excused not to follow Him saying that He was not attached to God!

With the same human nature He felt tired, hungry and suffering.

If He had not felt tired, hungry, thirsty or suffering, if He had not slept, it would not have been possible to say that He is the Son of Man and that He took what was ours, took the same nature sentenced to death so that He might in it die on our behalf and redeem man.

As God He was not tired because the Godhead is beyond fatigue.

It was the human nature which united with His Godhead and were not separated for one moment or a twinkling of an eye that felt tired because it accepts fatigue. The Lord Christ, so that His incarnation be an established fact able to carry out redemption, did not permit His divinity to prevent His humanity from being tired.

He did all this to pay off for our sins and atone for the sins of the people (Heb 2:1 7). We thank Him for bearing fatigue and pain for us.

With His fatigue He sanctified fatigue and every one is now rewarded according to his labor (1 Cor 3:8).

www.ingramcontent.com/pod-product-compliance
Lightning Source LLC
Chambersburg PA
CBHW071507040426
42444CB00008B/1531